HISTORY OF INVENTION

SHIPS AND SUBMARINES

SHIPS AND SUBMARINES

Chris Woodford

☑®

Facts On File, Inc.

Facts On File, Inc.
132 West 31st Street
New York, NY 10001

Library of Congress Cataloging-in-Publication Data

Woodford, Chris
    Ships and submarines / Chris Woodford.
        p. cm.
    Summary: Introduces the development of submarine and ship technology, from the dawn of civilization to the present, including Egyptian plank boats, ocean liners, and sports boats.
    Includes bibliographical references and index.
    ISBN 0-8160-5439-8
    1. Ships—Juvenile literature. 2. Submarines (Ships)—Juvenile literature. [1. Ships—History. 2. Submarines (Ships)—History.] I. Title.

VM150.W66 2003
623.8'2—dc22
                                              2003013447

Facts On File books are available at special discounts when purchased in bulk quantities for businesses, associations, institutions, or sales promotions. Please call our Special Sales Department in New York at (212) 967-8800 or (800) 322-8755.

You can find Facts On File on the World Wide Web at http://www.factsonfile.com

For The Brown Reference Group plc:
Project Editor: Tom Jackson
Design: Bradbury and Williams
Picture Research: Becky Cox
Managing Editor: Bridget Giles
Consultant: L. Scott Miller, Professor of Aerospace
    Engineering, Wichita State University, Kansas.

Printed and bound in Singapore

10 9 8 7 6 5 4 3 2 1

The acknowledgments on page 96 form part of this copyright page. Every effort has been made to contact copyright holders of any material reproduced in this book. Any omission will be rectified in subsequent printings if notice is given to the publishers.

CONTENTS

$35.00

BUOYANCY

Why do whales float in water while people, who are so much smaller and lighter, simply sink? How can a ferry carry dozens of trucks and automobiles across the sea when even one of those vehicles, by itself, cannot float? The answer to these questions is buoyancy: Some things float easily in water while others do not float at all.

We owe the science of buoyancy to Archimedes (287–212 B.C.E.), one of ancient Greece's best remembered mathematicians. Archimedes realized that things float if they weigh less than the same volume of water—an idea now known as Archimedes'

principle. Suppose you take a truck, measure its volume, and weigh it. Then you take an equal volume of water and weigh that. Because the truck is made mostly of iron, which is a very dense material, it weighs more than the same volume of water. That means a truck will sink in water. Now suppose you built a truck from wood that was exactly the same size as the metal one. That would weigh less than both a metal truck and the same volume of water, so it would float.

When an object floats, it does not remain on the surface but sinks partly into the water. Archimedes realized that a

Archimedes figured out why objects float or sink when he was taking a bath. He was thinking about ways of showing that a gold crown was actually made from less expensive metal. He realized he could measure an object's volume, and then its density, by collecting the water it displaced. This idea led him to develop his famous principle of buoyancy.

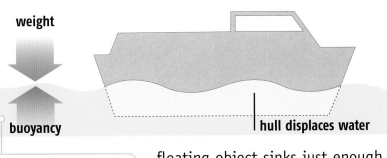

weight

buoyancy

hull displaces water

A ship stays afloat because it weighs less than the volume of water it displaces.

floating object sinks just enough so that it pushes aside (displaces) its own weight of water. A ship does not sink completely because the pressure of the body of water underneath it pushes it upward with a force called buoyancy. This buoyancy force is exactly equal to the ship's total weight (including the weight of its cargo). A ferry floats because it covers a large area of water. The buoyancy force of all that water under the ferry is enough to support its weight, even if it is made of metal.

From the smallest and most basic canoe, to the biggest oil tanker or most sophisticated cruise liner, the simple idea of buoyancy has made possible every ship and submarine ever built. In many ways, the history of ships and submarines is the story of how people mastered the science of buoyancy to take to the seas.

Fish and Submarines

How things work

Fish defy the usual laws of buoyancy: They can float and sink when they want to. They owe this remarkable ability to an organ inside their bodies called a swim bladder (or air bladder), which they can fill up at will with gases produced by their blood. Just as inflatable armbands help novice swimmers float, so a fish's swim bladder gives it more buoyancy than it would otherwise have. By regulating the amount of gas in its swim bladder, a fish can make itself float at a particular depth, rise to the surface, or sink to the bottom. Submarines use a similar idea. Instead of a swim bladder, they have tanks that can be filled with air (to make them rise) or water (to make them dive).

PREHISTORIC BOATS

A Canadian Inuit in a kayak on Arctic waters in 1914. The word kayak *means "hunter's boat." The first kayaks were built from seal skins and bone.*

It is surprising that we know a lot about the history of aircraft and little about the history of ships and boats, which are much older. While aircraft have been crisscrossing the sky for little more than a hundred years, the first boats took to the seas tens of thousands of years earlier. Indeed, boats are such an old idea that they go back even before the start of recorded history. Although prehistoric boats developed in different ways in different parts of the world, archaeologists believe all modern boats evolved from just four early craft: rafts, skin boats, bark boats, and dugouts.

RAFTS

No one knows who built the first boat or where and when they did so, but people probably floated down rivers on logs and rafts a long time ago. The idea to build a boat probably came from watching a piece of driftwood floating on the sea, and the first rafts were probably made from logs or bundles of reeds bound together.

Rafts are so simple that they can be made even without tools, so they could easily have been built by prehistoric peoples. Unlike other types of boats, which float because their hull, or bottom section, displaces water with its weight, by Archimedes' principle, rafts float simply because of the natural buoyancy of the logs (or other materials) from which they are made.

Rafts are quick and easy to build, but they have one big disadvantage: Unlike a boat with a built-up hull, rafts offer little protection from the sea. So waves wash over the top, drenching any passengers or cargo. Rafts tend to drift wherever the current takes them because, unlike most other boats, they are not shaped to move in any particular direction. They can, however, be paddled or sailed a long way across the sea, as Norwegian adventurer Thor Heyerdahl proved in the 1940s.

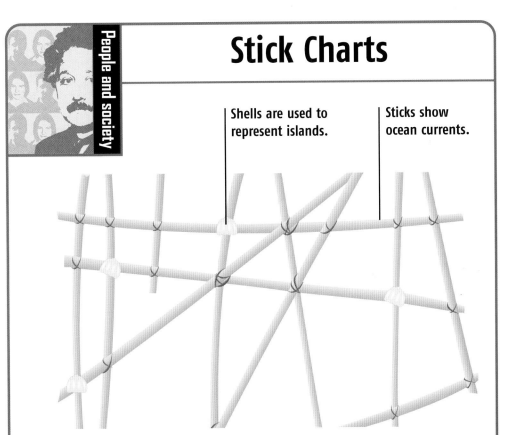

People and society

Stick Charts

Shells are used to represent islands.

Sticks show ocean currents.

Ancient seagoing peoples needed more than just vessels that could cross the ocean, they also needed ways of navigating (finding their way). Long before maps and compasses, sailors in Micronesia (a group of Pacific Ocean islands east of the Philippines) developed charts made of sticks (above) to find their way around and teach others about navigation. Coconut and sea shells represented the islands and sticks or palm fibers showed the ocean currents (swells) running between them. Just as maps can show more or less detail with different scales (amounts of detail), so stick charts were constructed in different sizes to represent larger or smaller areas. Charts called *mattang* showed the swells around one or two islands in great detail. *Meddo* charts showed more islands and fewer swells. *Rebbilib* charts concentrated mainly on showing how many different islands related to one another.

Coracle

The Welsh coracle is one of the world's oldest boat designs and is like a large floating basket. Since this photograph was taken in the 1900s, coracles have become much rarer.

1. The framework was woven from a light wood such as hazel or willow. The frame was then covered in animal skin and waterproofed with tar.

2. The seat is designed for one person who propels the coracle using a paddle.

3. The coracle is light enough for one person to carry the boat using a rope threaded through these strap holes.

SKIN BOATS

Ancient peoples found they could make another type of boat by covering a simple wood or bone skeleton with animal hides. Skin boats were probably invented by hunting peoples who found an ingenious new use for the parts of animals that they did not eat. Among the lightest of water-going vessels, skin boats are much too flimsy for use on the sea. Yet they are ideal for carrying one or two people up and down rivers and would have made good fishing boats for ancient hunters.

Skin boats are still built today in some parts of the world using traditional techniques handed down over thousands of years. One example is the Inuit kayak. This is made by stretching seal skins over a framework made of wood or whale bone and then waterproofing them with animal fat. Designed for hunting at speed, the kayak has a sleek pointed bow (front end) and stern (back end) that can carry one or two people. The *umiak* is a more rounded version of a kayak that was generally used by women for transporting things. Other common skin boats include the Welsh *coracle*. Shaped like a round bowl, these can be spun around and paddled in any direction. The *qaffa* is another rounded skin boat. Up to 18 feet (5.5 m) across, it could carry up to 20 passengers. It was popular on the Tigris and Euphrates Rivers in present-day Iraq and dates back many thousands of years.

BARK BOATS

Bark boats have a similar design to skin boats, but bark is thicker and less likely to be punctured than most animal skins. The bark is cut from tree trunks in long strips, which are stitched together with fibers made from tree roots. A lightweight internal structure made from a lighter wood is then built up inside it. While a skin boat gets its strength mainly from the internal skeleton, a bark boat owes most of its strength to the bark. A skin boat is made by stretching animal skin over a framework; but in a bark boat, the outer bark is shaped first and the framework is built last. The skin boat and the bark boat are both quite flimsy vessels suited only for traveling on calm inland waters. One of the biggest problems with both types of boat is the danger of a puncture in the skin or bark

A Native American constructs a canoe from birch bark in Ontario, Canada. Canoes are best suited to calm inland and coastal waters and were especially common on the many North American lakes.

How things work

Building a Dugout Canoe

Unlike rafts, which can be built in minutes or hours by lashing logs together, dugout canoes took months to build. A large tree of the right size and shape had to be found and felled. Before chainsaws or even handsaws had been invented, trees were often felled by setting fire to their base. Groups who lacked any means of chopping down large trees were limited to using trees that had already fallen to the ground. Once it had been chopped down, the tree had to be dried out and this alone could take three months or more. When the tree was completely dry, its inner wood was removed by setting fire to one small section at a time (right) and scraping out the burned remains with shells or other primitive hand tools.

layer, which would fill the vessel with water and sink it very quickly. The bark of many different types of trees was used to make these boats, although birch trees were especially popular in Europe and North America. In the Pacific Northwest, birch-bark canoes were made up to 46 feet (14 m) long.

DUGOUTS

As the name suggests, a dugout canoe was made by literally digging out the wood from a fallen tree to make a long, tree-shaped boat. The bow and stern may have been carved to a point to make the boat travel more swiftly through the water. Dugouts

are known to have been in widespread use in Europe around 10,000 years ago. Archaeologists have found many remains of dugout canoes buried in or near rivers. They are built from sturdy trees so they tend to survive much better than other types of boats.

In many ways, dugouts were the most superior of all the early boats. Their sturdiness set them apart from much more flimsy skin and bark boats. While rafts could be sturdy, too, the shaped hulls of dugouts were much more practical, especially in rough ocean water. Dugouts were also easier to steer. Perhaps most importantly of all, the base of a dugout canoe could be built up into a much more sophisticated vessel by adding extra pieces of wood on top. The basic design of dugout canoes has been used as the starting point for nearly all the modern ships and boats that have followed.

Key inventions

Ancient Shipyard

One reason we know about the boats of the past is that some of them still survive today: The water and mud of wetlands can preserve sturdy dugout canoes in excellent condition for thousands of years. In 2000, a group of environmental science students were out walking near Newnan's Lake in Gainesville, Florida, when one of them spotted the outline of a boat in the sand. Careful digging revealed a preserved dugout canoe, thousands of years old. A more thorough dig at the site revealed over 100 other canoes up to 31 feet (9 m) long (similar to above). It was the biggest collection of ancient canoes ever found in the United States. One clue to this find lies in the name of the lake. The native people call it Pithlachocco, which means "the place where boats are made." Archaeologists had found an ancient shipyard.

KON-TIKI MAN

Without historical records, the only sure way to prove what ancient peoples could have achieved is to try to repeat their feats ourselves using the tools and materials that would have been available in ancient times. This is what Norwegian adventurer Thor Heyerdahl (1914–2002) and the *Kon Tiki* expedition attempted in 1947.

While studying wildlife in the Polynesian islands of the South Pacific, Heyerdahl found himself wondering how the first settlers had arrived there. Up until that time, historians had always believed Polynesian people had arrived from Asia. Heyerdahl thought it was more likely that they had traveled east from South America, because that was the way in which the sea currents and winds tended to move. People were skeptical when Heyerdahl wrote a book about his idea, *American Indians in the Pacific*. So he decided to settle the issue by making the journey himself by raft.

That raft was *Kon Tiki*. It was built in Peru in 1947 using only materials from Ecuador that were available to South American Indians in ancient times. Nine balsawood

*The **Kon Tiki** sets out on the expedition in 1947. The flimsy raft survived many dangers, while at sea, and it was nearly lost as it was approaching land. The crew were unable to steer the raft very well and were lucky not to be dashed against the reef by huge waves as they tried to reach the shore.*

*Explorer Thor Heyerdahl steers the **Kon Tiki** during the 1947 expedition. This was his first of many adventurous voyages.*

The similarity between reed boats used in South America (left) and Arab craft led Heyerdahl to suggest that reed boats were used to cross the Atlantic. In 1970, Heyerdhal sailed Ra-2, a large reed ship, from Morocco to Barbados.

logs, lashed together with rope made a large platform about 45 feet (14 m) long and 18 feet (5.5 m) wide. The logs were covered in tough bamboo stalks to make a simple deck and a hut was built on top. Logs were also used to make the masts that supported square sails.

When Heyerdahl and his five colleagues set off from Callao, Peru, in 1947, few people expected the voyage would end in anything other than disaster. How could a flimsy raft hope to cross the Pacific Ocean, where even sturdy modern vessels were often lost in rough seas? The secret of *Kon Tiki's* survival lay in its very simple raft design. Sodden with water, its balsa logs moved up and down without chafing the ropes that held them together. It was small enough to ride huge waves and survived two storms. A raft cannot fill up with water; so when huge waves lashed over *Kon Tiki*, the water simply drained away through the deck.

Just 101 days after its departure, *Kon Tiki* arrived on the isolated reef of Raroia in Polynesia after a truly epic voyage. The distance from Callao to Raroia is about 4,000 miles (6,450 km), and the raft was helped along its way by swift ocean currents.

Heyerdahl wrote a book about his expedition. Many of his colleagues were doubtful about Heyerdhal's theories, but his ideas have been rediscovered in more recent years. A new generation of historians now believe that Heyerdahl was a visionary and that his ideas were way ahead of his time.

SHIPS IN ANCIENT TIMES

It was the ancient peoples of the Mediterranean who discovered how to travel farther and faster by building simple canoes into sturdy ocean-going vessels. Powered by oars and then sails, these often formidable ships were big enough to carry cargo and swift enough to wage war. The advances in shipbuilding technology swept ancient peoples over the seas to new lands.

EGYPTIAN ADVANCES
It was the ancient Egyptians who made the first major advance in shipbuilding around 3000 B.C.E.

Not content with the flimsy design of their simple reed boats, they discovered they could make bigger and better ships by building up a framework using planks of wood. Without the benefit of large trees, the Egyptians had to construct their vessels from thousands of small planks lashed together with rope made from grass. Historians think the Egyptians could have developed planking technology in one of two ways: They might have covered a reed boat with tarred cloth, added planks on top, and then removed the reeds afterward.

Tourists travel in **feluccas** *down the* **Nile River past tombs cut into the rocks at Aswan in Egypt. The felucca, a wooden sail boat, has been used to travel on the Nile since ancient times.**

Bow is shaped for ramming.

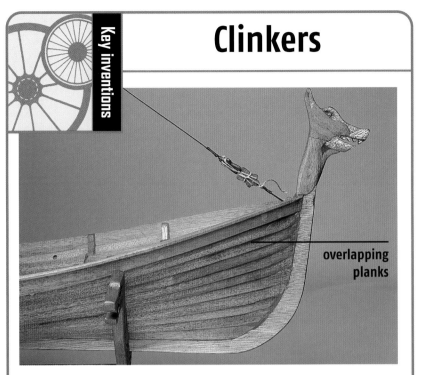

Clinkers

overlapping
planks

Up until the time of the Vikings, the hulls of wooden ships were built by fixing the bottom of each plank to the top of the plank beneath it. Around 300 C.E., the Vikings introduced lapstrake construction, or clinker building, in which the planks overlap slightly (above). In early clinker-built ships, the planks were lashed to the framework beneath them. Later they were fastened on by pegs and nails. Clinker ships have very strong hulls but they moved less swiftly through the water.

In about 700 B.C.E. the Phoenicians built fighting ships called biremes.

Shields protect the rowers.

Oars used to steer the ship.

Two banks of oars used for propulsion.

Or they might have fastened an outer plank structure to an internal wooden framework built on a simple dugout canoe.

Either way, the ships they constructed were remarkable pieces of engineering. By 2000 B.C.E., the Egyptians were making wooden ships more than 100 feet (30 m) long. Like reed boats, the first Egyptian plank boats were powered by oars. But the Egyptians made another important technological breakthrough when they added a simple bipod mast and sail. This was two poles joined at the top in a sturdy A-frame. Made of planks and driven by a single square sail, the largest cargo ships carried the huge blocks of stone, weighing many hundreds of tons, that were used by the Egyptians to build their monuments. Smaller ships were typically powered by a sail and a line of rowers on each side.

THE PHOENICIANS SET SAIL

Most Egyptian boats were built for use on the Nile River. Although they were much sturdier than reed boats, they were too flimsy for sailing out into the Mediterranean Sea. The Minoan people of Crete, however, were building seagoing ships about 2500 B.C.E. The Mycenaeans of Greece, pioneered basic sailing ships about a thousand years later. Yet it is the Phoenicians, who lived in an area that is now part of modern Lebanon, who made the first major voyages to the oceans beyond the Mediterranean around 1000 B.C.E. Their spectacular journeys were possible because they used sturdy "round boats." These were made from planks of cedar wood, with an internal structure of ribs and a keel. A keel is a central backbone that runs under the bottom of the boat from bow to stern. The Phoenicians ventured north to Britain and south as far as Africa in broad cargo ships powered by sails. Although they were traders more than they were warriors, the Phoenicians also pioneered the galley. A galley is any large, seagoing warship powered by oars or sails. The Phoenicians may have been the first people to develop biremes, or ships with two banks of oars, pulled by rowers sitting on two levels) and *triremes*, with three banks of oars.

GREEK GALLEYS WAGE WAR

The ancient Greeks drove ship technology forward through a number of important advances, and are now remembered primarily for their formidable warships. Greek ships often had a raised section at the front called a forecastle and a covered cabin at the back. Although the Greeks revolutionized the design of sails, their warships also had banks of oars similar to Phoenician biremes and triremes to give them extra speed and power. That became important when the Greeks added rams to the fronts of their vessels for smashing into enemy ships.

Key inventions

Dhows and Junks

A two-masted sailing boat called a *dhow* has been used in the Middle East since ancient times. This innovative sailing vessel has a raised deck at the stern and a sharp pointed bow. The dhow can move very swiftly under the power of its single large sail. It was used for trading between Africa, India, and Arabia and is still a common sight in parts of Africa and India. In China and Japan, flat-bottomed boats called *junks* (above) were developed toward the end of the first millennium and are still widely used today. They are easy to recognize, with unusual square sails mounted on bamboo poles that can be closed together. Unlike most other types of boats, junks have no keel (ridge along hull). Although this makes a boat harder to maneuver, junks overcome the problem by having a large, central rudder. They owe their great strength to huge internal braces known as bulkheads. These divide the hull into a number of watertight compartments and make a junk virtually unsinkable.

THE ROMAN FLEET

After the Greeks, it was the Romans who dominated the Mediterranean with the largest shipping fleet of ancient times. While powerful galleys helped them conquer new lands, huge cargo ships were needed to supply their sprawling empire, which lasted from 27 B.C.E. to 395 C.E.

Roman galleys had several innovations, including a bridge, a raised upper section at the front to make it easier to board enemy vessels, and catapults for firing missiles. Armor plating, often made from thick leather or cloth, protected the ships' hulls. The ships had large oars and a sail at the front that made the craft easier to maneuver when attacked. At up to 180 feet (55 m) long and 45 feet (14 m) wide, Roman cargo ships were mighty vessels even by modern standards. Used for ferrying grain and other goods from Egypt to Rome, they could carry about 1,100 tons (1,000 metric tons) of cargo and 1,000 passengers as well.

Roman Corbita

Roman cargo ships called *corbitas* traveled to all the ports of the Roman Empire. The hull was pear-shaped to make more room for cargo.

1. The helmsman steered the ship from the stern by dipping two large blades into the water.

2. The crossbeam, or yard, was called the *antenna* in Latin. This is were we get our word for a radio mast.

3. The cargo or passengers were loaded through a central hatch.

4. The hull was made from planks joined end to end.

The Power of Oars

Before shipbuilders had truly mastered the art of harnessing windpower with sails, they thought the best way to make ships move faster was to add more oars. But there was a limit to how long they could build their ships, so extra rowers had be added. They sat in rows, or banks, one on top of another.

Galleys containing two banks of oars were known as biremes and are thought to date back to sometime between

1700 and 600 B.C.E. Triremes (like this replica, below) had three banks of oars and were probably invented between 600 and 500 B.C.E. The Greeks and Romans both had *quadriremes* (four banks of oars) and *quinquiremes* (with five banks of oars). But historians are unsure whether the rowers in these larger ships sat in tiers pulling on their own oar, which would have made ships very high, or whether several people pulled on each oar on just one or two levels. Although later ships had even more banks of oars—the fabulous *tessaraconter* had 40 banks—so many rowers proved very cumbersome to organize and were eventually made obsolete by sailing ships.

VIKING CONQUESTS

Not all of the early developments in ship technology happened around the Mediterranean. Toward the end of the first millennium C.E., seafaring warriors from Scandinavia, known as Vikings, started to terrorize much of northern Europe in swift longships powered by oars and sails.

These sturdy vessels owed much of their strength to a type of construction called clinker building: The wooden planks were overlapped slightly instead of being joined edge to edge. Built for sailing the rough seas of the North Atlantic, longships also had reinforced bows and sterns. They carried up to sixty rowers on each side. Sometimes the Vikings set fire to their ships to repel invaders, or deliberately sank them to create a barricades against their enemies. When great Viking warriors died, they were cast adrift on a burning longship.

Not all the Viking ships were designed for waging war. They also built a cargo ship with a more rounded hull known as *knorr*, for example, which were powered by a single sail. Ships like this were steered by a single rudder attached to the right-hand side at the back. Known as a steer board, this gave rise to *starboard*, the word that sailors still use for the right side of a ship. The left side of a ship is known as *port* because the ship always docked on that side. It could not dock on the right because of the steer board.

SAILING THROUGH HISTORY

Although sails were first used in the ancient world, oars remained a more reliable way of powering ships, especially in battles, and were widely used until the late Middle Ages (about 1500 c.e.). But large numbers of rowers took up huge amounts of space and also needed food, so they limited how far a ship could travel and how much it could carry. Many ships of all periods combined the best of both worlds with banks of rowers and sails as well. Eventually, however, oar-powered vessels were replaced entirely by sailing ships.

THE FIRST SAILORS

Historians believe sails were invented in ancient Mesopotamia (now part of Iraq) around 7,000 years ago. The first real evidence of sailing ships comes from Egyptian paintings dating from around 3500 b.c, which show vessels with a single large square sail hanging from a bipod mast. The first Egyptian sails were taller than they were wide. Later, the Egyptians found that rectangular sails, wider than they were tall, caught the wind better. While ancient warships were powered by oars and sometimes had sails as

A modern-day copy (replica) of the sailing ship, the Santa María, which Italian explorer Christopher Columbus sailed on his voyage to America in 1493. In the background is the launch pad at the Kennedy Space Center, in Florida.

Egyptian Ship

Ancient Egyptians traveled in sailing ships on the Nile River.

1. The sail was made from linen or cloth. The wind generally blew upstream in Egypt, and sailors used their sails to travel in this direction.

2. The sail could be opened and closed by pulling on these many ropes.

3. Large oars were used to steer the ship back downstream with the river's current.

1

2

3

A painting showing Viking Erik the Red sailing from Iceland to Greenland in a tough longship in 982. His son, Leif Ericson, was one of the first Europeans to sail to North America in 1002.

well, transport ships needed much more space to carry cargo and were powered only by a sail.

The Egyptians, Minoans, Mycenaeans, Phoenicians, Greeks, Romans, and Vikings all used square sails, which were typically hung from a single large mast in the center of the ship. If winds caught such a big sail, they could sometimes snap the mast completely in half. This is why masts were tied to the bow and stern by several ropes to give them extra support. Although square sails worked fine when the wind blew from behind, they could not be used to sail directly into the wind: That would simply push the boat backward.

Fortunately, the problem of how to sail into the wind had already been solved in the Arab world, where dhows had pioneered a very different kind of sail shaped like a triangle. Known as a *lateen*, this type of sail is especially useful for sailing toward the wind and was used by Mediterranean peoples from around 200 C.E. onward.

A great advance in sailing came when the Greeks began to build ships with more than one mast and several different sails. First they added a second mast that sloped up from the bow and held a small square sail. Next they added a lateen sail on top of the main sail. And finally, they added another square sail at the stern. With more than one sail, ships could sail in winds from any direction—as generations of sailors have done ever since.

SHIPS IN THE MIDDLE AGES

Ancient ships were steered either by getting the rowers to row harder on one side than on the other or, if the craft was powered by sails, by using a large board mounted on one side that dipped in the water. Around 1200 C.E., sailing ships in the West began to copy the idea of using a central rudder to steer a ship. This was first used in Chinese junks. With rudders and a mixture of square and lateen sails, ships became much easier to control.

A number of popular ship designs emerged in the early Middle Ages, one of which was the *cog*. It was developed by the shipbuilders of northern Europe following the demise of the Vikings. This spacious ship had one large mast and was powered by a single square sail. Although used mainly as a cargo ship, it could also be used in battle. The bow and stern were built up to form high, castlelike structures from which the ship could be defended by archers against an enemy attack. Cogs also used the new idea of a rudder mounted on the stern for steering. Like tough Viking longships, cogs were designed to travel through the rough waters of the North Atlantic, so they were clinker built for added strength.

Cog

As this model shows, the cog had a large hull and could carry huge amounts of cargo.

1. The size of the square, main sail was linked to the size of the hull. As cog hulls became bigger, so did the sails.

2.Raised areas at the front and back of the ship made it easier to defend.

3. The rudder at the stern of the ship replaced steering oars.

4. A ridge, or keel, runs along the bottom of the ship, making it more stable in rough seas.

How things work

Into the Wind

Square sails can drive a ship forward, but only if the wind is coming more or less from behind. Only triangular (lateen) sails can be used to sail toward the wind (above). These sails work just like kites or wings. As the wind passes over their curved surface, it moves faster over the top than around the bottom. This generates a force called lift that rushes the boat forward into the wind. Clipper ships used square sails hung across their width and lateen sails hung along their length. This enabled them to catch winds from virtually any direction and sail directly into an oncoming wind.

While square-sailed cogs were being developed in northern Europe, shipbuilders around the Mediterranean had started to make more use of the triangular lateen sail. They also developed new ways of building wooden ships by constructing a keel and a solid framework of ribs and then adding the outer planked hull on top. These lateen-rigged ships, known as *lateeners*, were generally smaller and less sturdy than cogs. Cogs were clinker built, but lateeners had a hull made with planks that were joined smoothly together, so lateeners moved much more swiftly through the water. The joints between the planks were sealed with tar to prevent water from seeping through. This shipbuilding technique was not new; it was a more advanced version of the methods that people had used since ancient times. Ships called *caravels* were among the first to be built in this way. The method is known as carvel-building for this reason. Great explorers such as Italian Christopher Columbus (1451– 1506) and Portuguese Vasco da Gama (1460–1524), who traveled to India in the 1490s, made their voyages in caravels.

Cogs and lateeners had both helped to advance shipbuilding technology, but each had its advantages and drawbacks. Cogs were sturdy and spacious, but their single square sail was an inefficient and unreliable source of power. Lateeners were smaller and lighter, but their triangular sails made them better able to respond to changing winds. It was inevitable that the best features of cogs and lateeners would eventually be combined in a single ship design. Developed in 1400s, the *carrack* soon became the main cargo ship used in Europe. Like cogs, carracks had castles at the bow and stern, but they were designed for carrying cargo. Fitted with three masts and a mixture of square and lateen sails, these ships were both fast and maneuverable.

GALLEYS AND GALLEONS

Although cargo ships like the carrack became increasingly popular during the Middle Ages, galleys remained just as important as they had always been. Galleys were generally warships but they were also used for carrying cargo and passengers. Sailing power had advanced considerably since ancient times, but galleys continued to use oar power (as well as sails) right through the Middle Ages. A typical galley of the 13th century was the *tarida*, which could be powered either by

The Armada

The bold Spanish Empire finally over-reached itself in 1588 when King Philip II of Spain attempted to invade England with 130 galleons carrying around 30,000 troops. The Spanish believed this fleet, known as the *Armada*, was invincible, but the English navy attacked off the south coast of their country and forced the Spanish fleet to retreat. The Spanish galleons were large and slow. The British ships, by contrast, were smaller and sleeker. When the Armada anchored itself off the coast of France, the English attacked again and the Spanish fled. During the course of the battle the English set fire to ships and left them to float toward the Spanish fleet (above). A storm battered the surviving ships, and a little more than half of the Armada made it back to Spain. This defeat marked the end of Spain's dominance of the ocean.

Where in the World?

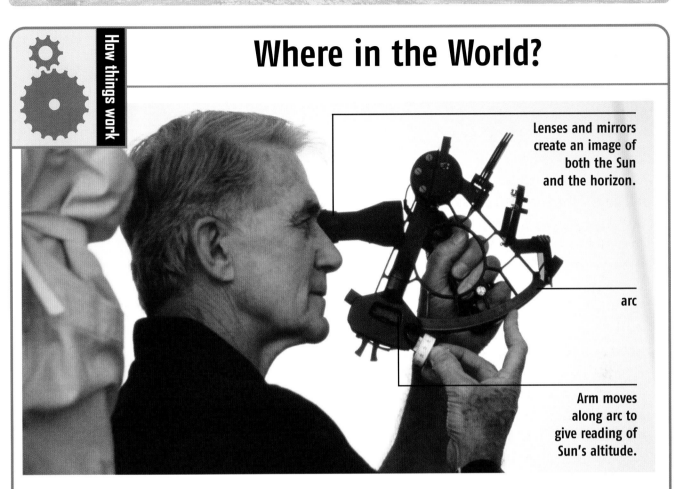

Lenses and mirrors create an image of both the Sun and the horizon.

arc

Arm moves along arc to give reading of Sun's altitude.

Many early sailors got lost easily if they moved out of sight of land. Those that did attempt long journeys across open water, guessed their position by monitoring the ship's direction and speed after they lost sight of land. This system is called dead reckoning and is far from effective. Navigators often used a magnetic compass, which had been invented in China in the 12th century, to show their direction, but they had to rely on inaccurate maps and guesswork. They measured speed by throwing a float over the side tied to a knotted rope. They counted the knots to estimate their speed. This is why the word *knot* is used to describe a ship's speed. A knot is 1 nautical mile (1.15 miles; 1.84 km) per hour.

In the 18th century, more accurate navigation systems were developed. Sailors began using sextants (above) to figure out their latitude—how far north or south they were. This device is used to measure the position of the Sun or other objects in the sky, such as the Moon and certain stars. With this information, sailors can look up their latitude on guide tables, called an almanac.

Also in the 18th century, people were devising systems to calculate longitude—the position east or west from a fixed point. The best system used accurate clocks called chronometers. One clock is set to a universal standard time based on the time at Greenwich, England, known as Greenwich Mean Time (GMT). The other clock tells the local time. Navigators have to reset this clock at noon every day. They know when it is noon by watching the Sun until it reaches its highest position in the sky. The difference between the two clocks gives the longitude. Every second of difference equals 1 nautical mile from Greenwich. The time in places to the east of Greenwich was ahead of GMT, while the time in places to the west is behind.

Having calculated both their longitude and latitude, navigators began to express their precise position degree (°) coordinates. The coordinates of St. Louis, Missouri, for example, are 39° north, 90° west. There are 180 degrees of latitude (90 north and 90 south) and 360 degrees of longitude (180 east and 180 west). A degree is divided into 60 "minutes," and a minute is 60 "seconds."

the sails hung from its twin masts or by the 150 rowers on board. The last type of galley to be built was the *galleas*, which was used in the 16th century. These ships were 150 feet (50 m) long and powered by three sails or up to 350 rowers pulling on 50 oars.

Galleys began to disappear toward the end of the 16th century, thanks to the arrival of a much more formidable vessel known as the *galleon*. Perhaps the best known of all the sailing ships, galleons had advantages over galleys: They were fully rigged with up to four masts and many different sails; they carried much heavier guns and more of them; they were usually powered only by sails, so they had more room for cargo; and with high stern castles, they had much more spacious living quarters. Galleons combined the best features of cargo ships and warships in a single vessel: They were big enough to carry huge cargoes around the world but also sturdy and well-equipped to fight in battles. Mighty galleons helped the Spanish conquer South America and carried gold and other treasures they plundered back to Europe. It was galleons that fought on both sides in one of the best known sea battles of all time, when a fleet of ships called the Spanish Armada tried to invade England in 1588.

In 1497, Italian explorer John Cabot sailed from England, to the island of Newfoundland, which he named. A full-sized copy of his ship The Matthew *made the same voyage in 1997. When compared to modern leisure boats and cars, the replica shows just how small the explorer's ship was.*

ships, the vessels that sailed on these lines were immensely successful. In 1818, the first transatlantic packet, or mail, service started carrying passengers and cargo between New York City and Liverpool, England. It took three to four weeks to cross from North America to England and six weeks to make the return journey.

Great competition developed between packet-ship operators. This is one reason why sailing ships became sleeker and faster in the 19th century. The fastest cargo ships of this time were the famous clippers. With slim and smooth carvel hulls and 30 or more square and lateen sails, they could speed through the water and they earned their name by "clipping off" the days or hours from a journey. The first vessels of this kind, known as Baltimore clippers, were developed in that U.S. city in the 1830s. Built in 1853, the biggest clipper was called the *Great Republic* and was built by famous Boston shipmaker Donald McKay (1810–80). Large clippers carried a huge area of sails—around 13,000 square feet (11,000 square m) or about twice the area of a baseball field!

Clippers and packet ships operated until the 1850s. Sail-powered vessels had carried explorers, traders, and soldiers to all corners of the world. But wood-planked ships were being replaced by iron ones, and sail power by steam. The age of powered vessels had arrived.

The British clipper **Cutty Sark** *was launched in 1869 to carry tea, but only made eight voyages as a tea clipper before being replaced by faster steamships.*

THE LAST SAILING SHIPS

As sea trade increased, shipbuilders developed faster and more reliable cargo vessels. Until the 19th century, ships had set sail only in favorable weather and only when they were fully loaded. But in 1814, merchants started a regular service between Albany and New York City whether the ship was full or not. Known as packet

INSIDE A SAILING SHIP

Sailing ships are made from a huge number of different pieces, each of which has its own name. The backbone of a ship is the keel, which runs under the vessel from the bow at the front of the ship to the stern at the back. Large upright posts built up from the keel at the bow (the stempost) and stern (the sternpost) added extra strength. Curved ribs stick outward from the keel, while beams run the length of the ship. At the top of each side, long curved beams known as gunwales (or gunnels) provide extra strength. Inside the ship, horizontal decks support the cargo or crew.

Other components are added to this basic structure. The forecastle (or fo'c'sle) is the raised section at the bow, while the sterncastle is usually a higher and larger area at the rear of the boat. The crew are housed inside the sterncastle. At the back of the ship, a rudder is attached to the sternpost.

The other vital part of a sailing ship is the arrangement of masts and sails, known as the rig. The net-like ropes that sailors climb up to adjust the sails is known as the rigging. Each of the masts has a different name. The main mast is at the center of the ship, the foremast at the bow, and the mizzen mast at the stern. However, ships could have as many as five or six masts. Horizontal beams called yards are attached to the masts. Sails are tied to the beam ends, known as yardarms. At the front there is usually a forward-sloping mast known as the bowsprit.

Sails were made from heavy canvas and are deliberately meant to hang loosely so the wind can catch them and drive the ship more efficiently. The numerous sails on a ship are all named according to where on the mast they are. The lowest sail is called the foresail or mainsail. Next comes the topsail, then the topgallant. Triangular lateen sails have other names. The sails that hang between the bowsprit and the foremast are known as jibs. Even the parts of a sail had their own names. For example, the corners of a lateen sail were called the peak, tack, and clew.

An upturned wooden ship frame being put together in a traditional shipyard. The curved ribs and horizontal beams will eventually be covered by a wooden hull.

Galleon

The galleon was a sleek warship. It was fast because of its large number of sails. Galleons were the fastest ships afloat in the 15th and 16th centuries. Their long, thin shape meant more cannons could be mounted along the side. The heavier guns were kept lower down in the ships so that they did not make the vessels top heavy. The cannons were fired through holes in the hull called *gunports*.

1. Topgallant sail

2. Topsail

3. The crew kept a look-out from the fore tops.

4. Mainsail

5. Bowsprit mast

6. Forecastles

7. Rigging

8. A bladelike structure at the bow, known as the *gripe*, cut quickly through the water.

9. Main mast

10. Jibsails were set at right angles to the other sails to catch winds blowing from the side.

11. The sterncastle had two sections. The upper part was called the poop deck, the lower part the quarterdeck.

12. The captain and officers lived in the rear section of the sterncastle, under the poop deck.

13. The word *galleon* may take its name from the balcony or gallery that runs along the stern.

14. The quarterdeck was the larger deck in the sterncastle.

15. Rudder for steering

OCEAN MACHINES

The Industrial Revolution began in Britain toward the end of the 18th century. It spread to other European nations and the United States over the next 50 years. Apart from changing the way goods were manufactured, the Industrial Revolution brought new ways to transport goods around the world. Steam engines powered by coal were soon driving mighty ships built from iron and steel— tough and versatile materials used in this new industrial age.

THE POWER OF STEAM

Rowers took up space and sails needed wind; there seemed to be no way of powering a ship that did not have any drawbacks. All that changed in 1712, when the English blacksmith Thomas Newcomen (1663–1729) invented the steam engine and Scottish engineer James Watt (1736–1819) turned it into a practical source of power about 50 years later. Steam engines were first used to pump water from mines. When they were later adapted for use in railroad locomotives, it soon became apparent that they could drive many other kinds of machines.

The first person to power a boat with a steam engine was a French nobleman called the Marquis d'Abbans (1751–1832). In 1783, he ran a steam-powered boat

Men shovel coal to produce steam power in the engine room of the USS Mississippi. One of the U.S. Navy's first steam vessels, the USS Mississippi fought in the Mexican War (1847) and the American Civil War (1861–65).

Pyroscaphe, *Greek for "fire boat," on its historic voyage in 1783. The steam engine gave out after 15 minutes.*

Despite its speed, the steamboat Clermont *was difficult to maneuver and it was frequently hit by other boats on the Hudson River.*

called the *Pyroscaphe* on France's Saône River. Three years later, U.S. inventor John Fitch (1743–98) developed the first American steamboat. When he failed to win backing from the government, he turned instead to private investors. Fitch eventually launched his 45-feet (14-m) ship on the Delaware River in 1787. The investment paid off when he later won the right to operate steamship services in the states of New York, Delaware, New Jersey, and Pennsylvania. Another pioneer of American steamboats was Robert

Fulton (1765–1815). In August 1807, his North River Steamboat, better known as the *Clermont,* ran the 150 miles (240 km) from New York City to Albany in just under a day and a half. That was less than half the time it took by sailboat. It was an impressive example of the power of steam. The *Clermont* became the first regular steamship service in the United States.

Steamships were soon venturing out from rivers onto the open seas. In 1819, the *Savannah* became the first steamship to cross the Atlantic Ocean, in a voyage lasting just over 30 days. The *Savannah* could carry only 80 hours worth of fuel, so it had to rely on sails for most of its journey. Despite its propulsion system, the *Savannah* was no faster than sail-powered packet ships, which made the same voyage in about a month. It was almost 20 years before regular steamship services began ferrying passengers across the Atlantic,

Propellers and Rudders

A ship's propeller is a bit like a windmill working in reverse. In a windmill, moving air blows past a set of huge blades. As they turn around, they spin the axle to which they are attached and provide the power to drive machinery inside the mill. In a ship, the engine turns the propeller and makes the blades spin around. This produces a backward-moving jet of water that moves the ship forward. Propellers are also known as screws because they moving through water like metal screws move through wood. The most efficient way to steer a boat is not simply to turn the rudder, but to change the direction in which the jet of water leaves the propeller. This is why a ship's rudder is placed immediately behind the propeller (far right): The water leaves the propeller, hits the rudder, moves off at an angle, and thus causes the ship to turn to one side.

straight rudder

Current of water propels the boat forward.

rudder facing right

Current of water pushes boat to the right.

Boat moves to the left.

rudder facing left

The rudder is used to steer the ship. When the rudder is straight the ship moves forward. Pulling the rudder to the left or right changes the direction of the current.

in April 1838. Two British ships made the first crossings at almost the same time. In 1837, the *Great Western*, built specifically for making the Atlantic crossing, traveled from Bristol, England, to New York City in 18 days. A year later the paddlewheeler *Sirius* went from Cork, Ireland, to New York City in just 15 days. Sail-powered clipper ships, however, remained faster than steamships for some time. In the 1850s, a 260-foot (79-m) clipper called the *James Baines*, built by Donald McKay, set a record by crossing from Boston to the English port of Liverpool in only 12 days.

From the *Pyroscaphe* to the *Great Western*, all the early steamships had been pushed

through the water by huge rotating paddle wheels mounted either on their sides or at the stern. Although they were simple pieces of engineering, paddle wheels were not very effective at driving a ship forward because they were only half submerged in the water. In 1804, American railroad pioneer and inventor

modern screw propeller. The first large vessel to try out this new form of propulsion was the *Great Britain*, which successfully crossed the Atlantic in 1845 but was also fitted with masts and sails.

THE AGE OF IRON

The *Great Britain* had another claim to fame: It was also the first iron-hulled ship to make a transatlantic voyage. Iron was being used in new ways during the Industrial Revolution, but in 1845 it was hardly a new discovery for shipbuilders. As far back as 1777, the first boat with a hull made completely out of iron had been built in Yorkshire, England. There was, however, a major problem with iron: It rusted quickly and fell apart when it came into contact with water. Shipbuilders remained unconvinced until 1787 when the English industrialist John Wilkinson (1728–1808), who had constructed the world's first iron bridge, built an iron barge.

Strong though wood was, it could not be used to build ships much longer than about 300 feet (90 m). One of the great advantages of iron was that it could, in theory, be used to build ships of any length. This was demonstrated spectacularly by the great British inventor and engineer Isambard Kingdom Brunel (1806–59), who constructed two mighty iron ships in the middle of the 19th century. One of these was the 322-foot (93-m) propeller-driven

John Stevens (1749–1838) had developed a way of powering a steamship with two propellers, although he soon abandoned the idea. It was more than 30 years later, in 1836, that both the English inventor Francis Pettit Smith (1808–74) and the Swedish engineer John Ericsson (1803–89), working separately, invented the

Composite Ships

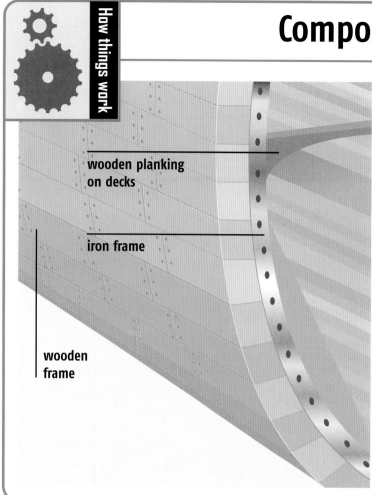

wooden planking
on decks

iron frame

wooden
frame

It took a long time to convince shipbuilders that iron was a suitable material for their vessels. Although stronger and longer-lasting, iron is a much less flexible material than wood. This proved to be a serious drawback, especially for iron sailing ships such as the last of the clippers. When heavily laden wooden ships were tossed about in rough seas, their creaking wooden structures helped absorb some of the sea's energy, in the same way, the springy suspension on an automobile helps smooth out the bumps in a road. But iron ships were tough and rigid and were thrown about much more by the sea since they could not absorb its energy. Sometimes their masts and rigging snapped entirely. Iron sailing ships solved the problem by reducing the amount of rigging. The problem disappeared in later iron steamships, which dispensed with masts and sails altogether.

Great Britain. This ship ran aground off the coast of Ireland in 1846. It was abandoned there for an entire winter but was later refloated with little damage. This was a powerful demonstration that iron was a more versatile material than shipbuilders had originally supposed. Brunel built an even bigger iron ship called the *Great Eastern* in 1858. That project was less successful, however, and proved to be Brunel's downfall.

It took many years for iron ships to replace wooden ones entirely. For a time, the two materials were used side by side—often together in the same ships.

In the 1850s, British ship designer John Jordan developed the composite ship, in which the inner framework was made of strong iron girders but the outer hull was built from traditional wooden planks.

The strength of iron and the flexibility of wood was a winning design. Many sail-powered clipper ships, including the record-breaking *Cutty Sark*, came to be built in this way.

THE EVOLUTION OF ENGINES

Few inventions are perfect when they are first introduced and steam engines were no exception.

Numerous improvements made to railroad steam engines soon found their way into ships.

In a steam engine, hot steam is produced by a boiler, which is like a large kettle. The steam is allowed to expand and push against a piston inside a separate cylinder. Single-acting steam engines, in which the piston is driven by steam in only one direction, were soon replaced by double-acting ones, In those engines, the pistons are driven in both directions. By the 1870s engines with just a single cylinder driving a single piston were becoming rarer. Most new ships were fitted with much more powerful compound engines, with two or more cylinders driving a piston each. New kinds of engines were also developed that used the waste steam from one cylinder to drive a second cylinder (a double-expansion engine) or even a third one (a triple-expansion engine). These and other innovations helped make steam engines much more efficient, so they produced more power for each ton of coal, and greatly reduced the amount of coal ships had to carry.

Despite these improvements, typical steam engines were seldom more than about 30 percent efficient—they wasted 70 percent of the energy they consumed.

The Great Eastern had two huge steam engines powered by ten boilers. The larger engine drove the propeller. The second powered the ship's two giant paddle wheels. The ship could reach a speed of 16 mph (25 km/h), but it was agreed that the engines were not powerful enough for such a huge vessel.

Turbines and Turbinia

Toward the end of the 19th century, the steam engine was given a new lease on life by Sir Charles Parsons (1854–1931) with his invention of the steam turbine. When Parsons installed three steam turbines in his 100-foot (30-m) motorboat *Turbinia* in 1897, it raced along at up to 40 mph (64 km/h). Even modern boats find it difficult to go this fast.

In a conventional steamship, one or more cylinders drive pistons up and down. Using an elbow-type joint known as a crankshaft, the pistons turn a wheel that drives the ship's paddle wheels or propeller. Something quite different happens in a steam turbine: A jet of high-pressure steam flows continuously past a set of fan blades, turning them around like the air passing over a windmill. Because the shaft to which the blades are attached is driven all the time, this is a much more powerful and efficient form of engine.

One drawback of steam turbines is that they turn at very high speeds, while a propeller needs to turn much more slowly to push a boat forward efficiently. Mechanical devices called reduction gears convert the high-speed rotations of the turbine to lower speeds for the propeller.

Steam turbines are also used to generate electricity, which is then used to power electric motors that turn the ship's propellers. Known as *turboelectric drive*, this form of ship power became popular after World War I (1914–18) and is still widely used today.

This was the main reason why inventors began developing engines that used a range of fuels at the end of the 19th century. In 1884, British engineer Charles Parsons developed a engine called a steam turbine, which was used to power the largest ships of the day. However, it was the gasoline and diesel engines that really sealed the fate of steam, being more suitable for smaller vessels. A steam engine is an external-combustion engine because the heat energy is produced by burning (combusting) coal outside (external to) the cylinder. Diesel and gasoline engines work by internal combustion: The fuel is burned inside the cylinder, wasting less energy.

German inventor Gottlieb Daimler (1834–1900) successfully powered a boat with a gasoline engine in 1886. Sixteen years later, in 1902, a French ship called *Petit Pierre* was the first boat to move under the power of a diesel engine. The following year, the *Wandal*, a boat on the Volga River in Russia, became the first large ship to use diesel propulsion. The first oceangoing diesel ship was the Danish *Selindia*, which made its maiden voyage in 1912.

Efficient new forms of power, from better steam engines to steam turbines and diesel engines, made it possible for ships to travel farther. Cargo could now be transported faster than ever before. Passengers, too, had the opportunity to travel the world in large and luxurious ships. Steam engines had totally revolutionized travel by sea, and the age of the ocean liner had arrived.

The Savannah *was powered by sail or steam. The paddle wheels, powered by a steam engine, were removed and laid on the deck when the sails were fully rigged.*

GREAT EASTERN

No ship was a better example of the spirit of the Industrial Revolution than the *Great Eastern*. It was the biggest steamship of its time and the forerunner of the huge cruise liners. Perhaps no one would have dared build such a vessel but the greatest naval architect of the age—English engineer Isambard Kingdom Brunel (1806–59).

By the time the *Great Eastern* was completed, in 1858, Brunel (right) had made his name building the Great Western Railway—a railroad that crossed the southwest of England. Following that early success, he started building huge steamships. In 1837, his *Great Western* paddlesteamer was the first iron vessel to cross the Atlantic. In 1845,

his *Great Britain* was the first propeller-driven vessel to make the same journey.

The *Great Eastern* was a major feat of engineering. At 692 feet (211 m) long and 82 feet (25 m) wide, it was about three times the size of the *Great Western* and took about five years to build. It had three different sources of power. Six masts carried 6,500 square yards (5,430 square m) of sails. Two large paddle wheels, one on either side, were powered by four boilers. The ship also had two huge propellers powered by six boilers. Five boiler rooms belched smoke out from five gigantic smokestacks.

Brunel had wanted the *Great Western* to carry up to 4,000 passengers and freight

Great Eastern

Brunel's *Great Eastern* was five times larger than any other ship at the time of its launch in 1858. It was so big it had to be launched sideways into the Thames River in London.

1. The hull was made from two layers of iron and was divided into ten watertight compartments. These compartments saved the boat from sinking on more than one occasion.

2. Masts meant that the ship could be totally powered by sails.

3. The two large paddle wheels measured 58 feet (18 m). *The Great Eastern* was the only ship in the world to have both paddle wheels and propellers.

4. Smoke from the ships 100 coal-fueled furnaces escaped through the five huge funnels.

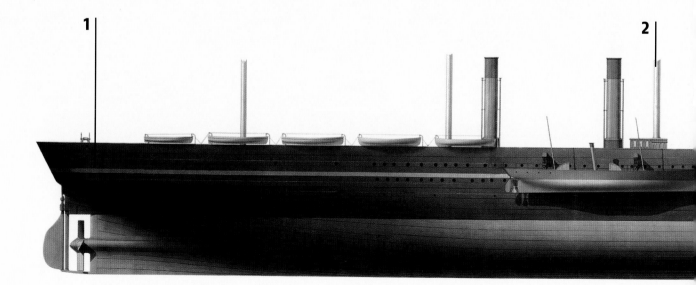

1

2

between Britain, Australia, and China, but things went wrong almost from the start. The ship cost around twice as much to build as originally expected and took several attempts to launch. One of Brunel's men was killed in the process. Brunel (left; with the ship's anchor chain) was the next casualty. The huge project drained him and ruined his health. On the eve of the *Great Eastern's* maiden voyage in 1858, he suffered a stroke (brain damage) and died a few months later.

In the years that followed the ship was a commercial flop and was soon withdrawn from service as a transport vessel. It briefly achieved fame again in the 1860s, when it was used to lay the first transatlantic telegraph cables. But by 1886 it had become a floating funfair in the port of Liverpool. It was scrapped three years later.

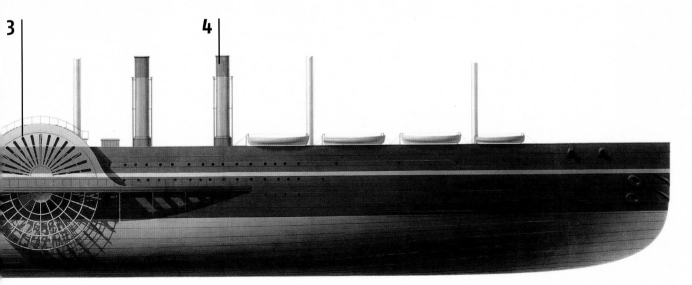

THE OCEAN LINERS

When Brunel started work on the *Great Eastern*, the first great ocean liner, its dockyard quickly became a tourist attraction. A huge crowd of 10,000 people paid to watch the vessel being launched in 1857. During the last half of the 19th century and the first half of the 20th century, few things captured people's imagination quite so much as the romance of ocean travel.

PEOPLE TAKE TO THE SEAS

Traveling by sea was far from a new idea. The large cargo ships built by the Romans could carry around 1,000 people. The idea of a passenger ship did not exist at

that time, however. There were simply warships and cargo ships, which carried passengers either in the cargo hold or on the open deck. It was the packet ships, launched in the early 19th century and sailing to regular timetables, that first made it practical and convenient for people to travel by ship. But the sea remained a perilous place. Wooden sailing ships frequently sank on longer voyages, carrying passengers down to the seabed with them. This earned many of them the macaber nickname "coffin ships." When the Industrial Revolution brought sturdy iron ships powered by steam, visionaries such as

Queen Elizabeth 2 (QE2) is the last passenger liner to make regular voyages across the Atlantic between the United States and Britain.

Isambard Kingdom Brunel sensed that many people would want to travel by sea, and the ocean liner was born.

LINERS AND LINES
Although Brunel's *Great Eastern* never fulfilled its promise, other ocean liners were more successful. That was partly due to the shipping lines (operating companies) that began to run them. At first, transatlantic services were provided only by the famous British companies Cunard and White Star Line. Later, German, French, and Dutch lines provided rival services. Around 100 liners were launched from 1850 through 1950. Glamorous and luxurious inside, most also had strong steel hulls outside that could easily withstand the dangers of the Atlantic. Such mighty

Ships of Steel

The great liners were made of steel. Steel is an alloy (mixture) of iron and carbon. It is much stronger than iron alone. Ocean liners were not the first steel ships, however. Even some sailing ships were built of steel in the second half of the 19th century. In the United States, for example, ships were built from steel from the 1880s on.

The hull of a steel ship is made of steel plates that are fixed to the framework underneath (above). In the first steel ships, these plates were joined together with small bolts called rivets that were banged in by hand. Later, rivets were added mechanically. Finally, during the 1930s, rivets were replaced by welding, where plates are melted together by high temperature gas or electric torches. This means the hull is effectively one large piece of steel, so it is both lighter, stronger, and smoother than an iron or wooden hull.

Wooden and iron ships were put together like a jigsaw in a dry dock. Near to a port, dry docks can be flooded and then emptied of water to repair a ship. Modern steel ships can be put together in much larger pieces that are themselves made either at a steel mill or elsewhere.

vessels inspired people's confidence and transformed the ocean voyage from perilous journey into romantic adventure.

Many of the liners were built by Britain and Germany at the end of the 19th century and the beginning of the 20th, as these two nations and their empires vied to dominate the world. Launched in 1906, the *Mauretania* was one of the first liners to take advantage of the newly developed steam turbine engine. It remained one of the fastest ships in the world for over 20 years. Built out of steel, *Mauretania* was funded partly with a loan from the British government, on condition that Britain could use it during any future war. Its sister ship, the *Lusitania,* was constructed under the same agreement. It met a tragic end in 1915 when a German submarine sank it during World War I, killing 1,200 of the people on board. Most liners built around this time had space for about 2,000 to 3,000 passengers.

After World War I ended in 1918, many more liners took to the seas. Some, such as the *Imperator*, were German ships that had been seized by the British or Americans during the long conflict. Others were groundbreaking vessels that set new standards in engineering and passenger comfort. When the French electric-powered ocean liner *Normandie* was launched in 1932 it was the first ship to be more than 1,000 feet (305 m) long. Two other transatlantic

ocean liners were launched the same decade. The British *Queen Mary* and *Queen Elizabeth* were about the same size as the *Normandie,* and they cut the time taken to cross the Atlantic to as little as four days.

Since air travel became widely affordable in the 1950s, few people have wanted to cross the Atlantic by ship—except for the pleasure of the experience. Today, only one great liner remains in service on the transatlantic route. Launched in 1967, Britain's *Queen Elizabeth 2* carries a maximum of 2,000 people at speeds of up to 33 mph (53 km/h). Its original steam engines were replaced with diesel in the 1980s to save fuel.

The huge liner Mauretania *had 25 boilers to provide steam for its turbine engines. The ship is pictured alongside a much smaller vessel, called* Turbinia. Turbinia *was the first ship to be powered by a steam turbine. It paved the way for fast liners like the* Mauretania.

Ship Beautiful

Launched in 1913 and nicknamed "Ship Beautiful," the British liner *Aquitania* was the grandest ship of its time. Its interiors (left) were copied from some of England's finest mansions. Its dining room had wooden beams and oak paneling in the style of a manor house. And with an open-air veranda, the Palm Lounge captured all the grace of an English country house. The *Aquitania's* finest room was its restaurant, decorated in the sumptuous style of the 18th-century French King Louis XVI. While its companion ships, the *Lusitania* and *Mauretania*, had been built for their speed, the *Aquitania* was unashamedly a ship of luxury.

TITANIC

When 100,000 people gathered to watch the launch of the ocean liner *Titanic* on May 31, 1911, none of them imagined that it would sink less than a year later, on its very first voyage, with the loss of more than 1,500 lives.

Unlike many other ocean liners before it, the *Titanic* had been designed mainly for safety and comfort. Made from steel plates joined together by rivets, it was 853 feet (260 m) long and 93 feet (28 m) wide. Power came from the eight-cylinder engines and steam turbines, which drove three huge propellers.

One of the *Titanic's* key features, however, was a hull divided into 16 watertight compartments by bulkheads. The ship's designers described the *Titanic* as "practically unsinkable," and they were confident that the ship could remain afloat if two of the compartments flooded with water; they even believed she might survive if four were flooded. They were wrong, as over 2,220 people on board the vessel discovered on the night of April 14, 1912. Just before midnight, the *Titanic* struck an iceberg off the coast

*Sketches made by a survivor sitting on an up-turned lifeboat show how the mighty **Titanic** broke up and sank in less than two hours.*

STRIKES STARBOARD BOW -12⁵ᵗ A.M.   11⁴⁵ P.M.

FORWARD END FLOATS, THEN SINKS   1.50 A.M.

SETTLES BY HEAD - BOATS ORDERED OUT   12⁰⁵ A.M.

STERN SECTION PIVOTS AMIDSHIPS AND SWINGS OVER SPOT WHERE FORWARD SECTION SANK.   2.00 A.M.

SETTLES TO FORWARD STACK   1.40 A.M.

LAST POSITION IN WHICH "Titanic" STAYED 5 minutes before   L.P. Skidmore.

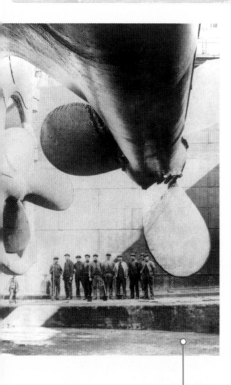

Bulkheads

How things work

Bulkheads are strong internal walls that divide the inside of a ship, below the waterline, into watertight compartments. If the hull is damaged and water starts to enter, only one compartment will flood. Water will not enter the other compartments, which will keep the ship afloat. First used in Chinese junks, bulkheads were recognized as a major advance in ship design by the great Italian explorer Marco Polo (c.1254–1324). He praised bulkheads that could keep a ship afloat "...if she springs a leak by running against a rock or on being hit by a hungry whale." It was not until the 19th century that bulkheads were generally used outside Asia.

*The **Titanic** was fitted with three huge propellers, one on each side and one in the center. They weighed 38 tons (42 metric tons) each.*

of Newfoundland, Canada. In a collision that lasted about 10 seconds, almost half of the ship's hull was damaged as it scraped past the iceberg. Rivets were torn out and the hull's steel plates opened up. Six of the watertight compartments were damaged and five immediately flooded with water. It soon became obvious to the captain and

crew that the *Titanic* was going to sink. Passengers were ordered on to the deck of the ship and put aboard lifeboats. But there were only enough of the small rowboats for half the people on the ship, and in the panic many of the lifeboats set off half empty. The *Titanic* sent out distress calls, but the nearest

ship, the *California*, had its radio turned off. Another liner, the *Carpathia* altered course to help. By the time it arrived at 4.30 A.M. the *Titanic* had been completely underwater for more than two hours. The *Carpathia* took 705 survivors on board, but 1,515 people died in one of the worst disasters in history.

*The **Titanic** was thought to be so safe that it was equipped with 20 lifeboats intended to save passengers from other sinking ships.*

SHIPS OF TODAY

Although airplanes have captured much of the passenger shipping market, billions of tons of goods are still shipped across the ocean each year on cargo vessels. There are roughly 44,000 large ships afloat today. Most of them fall into one of four types: tankers, bulk carriers, general cargo ships, and container vessels.

TANKERS

From the 1850s to the 1950s, ocean liners were the biggest ships to set sail. But after that period, there was a dramatic increase in the amount of oil produced and consumed by the world. Oil tankers soon became the biggest vessels. One of the first tankers was the steam-powered *Gluckauf*, built in Britain in 1886. It weighed 3,020 tons (2,718 metric tons). Tankers gave way to even bigger vessels called supertankers. The world's biggest tanker, and the largest ship of any kind, is currently the *Jahre Viking*. At 564,650 tons (508,185 metric tons), it is almost 200 times heavier than the *Gluckauf*. Its 1,500-feet (457-m) hull is about the same length as 80 cars parked bumper-to-bumper.

An oil tanker is little more than a floating gasoline can. With its engine and crew quarters located at the end of the stern, its hold is taken up by a set of gigantic oil tanks. These are separated from one another by bulkheads that run the length and breadth of the ship. Following a number of environmentally damaging oil spills, oil tankers are now built with one hull inside another (double hulls) to reduce the risk of them losing their cargo at sea.

BULK CARRIERS

Bulk carriers are similar to tankers in many ways. Both types of vessels are designed to carry only one kind of cargo at a time. While tankers carry liquids, bulk carriers transport solid goods such as coal, grain, sand, or sugar. Just like a tanker, a bulk carrier devotes most of its hull to the cargo hold. The engine room and bridge, where the captain and crew operate the ship are at the stern. Just like

People and society

Exxon *Valdez*

Oil tankers can quickly become disasters at sea when they run aground and spill their load. One of the worst tanker disasters of recent times happened on March 24, 1989, when the Exxon oil company's tanker *Valdez* struck a reef in Alaska and lost 12 million gallons (44 million liters) of crude oil. Although it was not the biggest oil spill ever seen, it happened in an area that was a haven for wildlife. The Exxon *Valdez* disaster (left) is estimated to have killed more than 1,000 sea otters and 34,000 sea birds and polluted 500 square miles (1,200 square km). The oil company, Exxon, was later fined $150 million and ordered to pay $1 billion to clean up the polluted area.

modern oil tankers, bulk carriers have grown enormously in size during the second half of the 20th century.

Bulk carriers are sometimes known as tramp ships. Liners make regular voyages between the same ports on a fixed schedule. Tramp ships, however make one-off voyages between any two places only when necessary. One week they might be carrying sugar, but on their return voyage, they might be shipping grain. Only crude raw materials tend to be shipped in this way. Finished goods are usually carried by liner service on container ships.

CONTAINER SHIPS

A container ship is quite different from any other kind of cargo vessel since the goods it transports are held inside large rectangular boxes. These metal containers can be loaded and unloaded from one ship to another, switched to trucks or railroad cars for journeys over land, or even carried aboard planes. This is possible because the containers used throughout the world are made to be exactly the same size. Containers measure 20 feet by 8 feet by 8 feet (6.1 m by 2.4 m by 2.4 m).

Container ships are a recent development in the world of shipping. The first one, the

Grain is poured directly into the vast cargo holds of a bulk carrier. These ships also carry passengers.

Container ships waiting to be loaded with cargo in a British dockyard.

Ideal X, was launched from Newark, New Jersey, in 1956 with just 58 containers on board. Today's mighty container ships carry over 6,600 containers, and the world's biggest container ship, the *Hamburg Express*, can hold up to 7,500. Typically more than 1,100 feet (335 m) long, the biggest container ships are known as post-Panama vessels because they are too large to pass through the Panama Canal, the narrow shipping lane that links the Atlantic and Pacific Oceans. Shipbuilders are currently

Key inventions

Smoother Cruiser

Launched in 1999, the world's biggest cruise ship, *Voyager of the Seas* (above), is almost like a floating town. It is 1,020 feet (310 m) long and 157.5 feet (48) wide. There is space for 3,100 passengers in the ship's 1,500 luxury cabins. Onboard entertainments include a theater, fitness center, skating rink, and street fair. Together, three huge dining rooms seat over 1,800 people. A crew of 1,181 keeps things running smoothly on the vessel as it sails back and forth between the Caribbean and Florida.

Lifeboats Inside and Out

Crew throw this line to people in the water. The line is attached to a float to make it easier to get hold of.

The coxswain (captain) gets the best view from the upper deck.

In the roughest weather, the coxswain steers from the bridge.

This life raft opens out automatically when it hits the water.

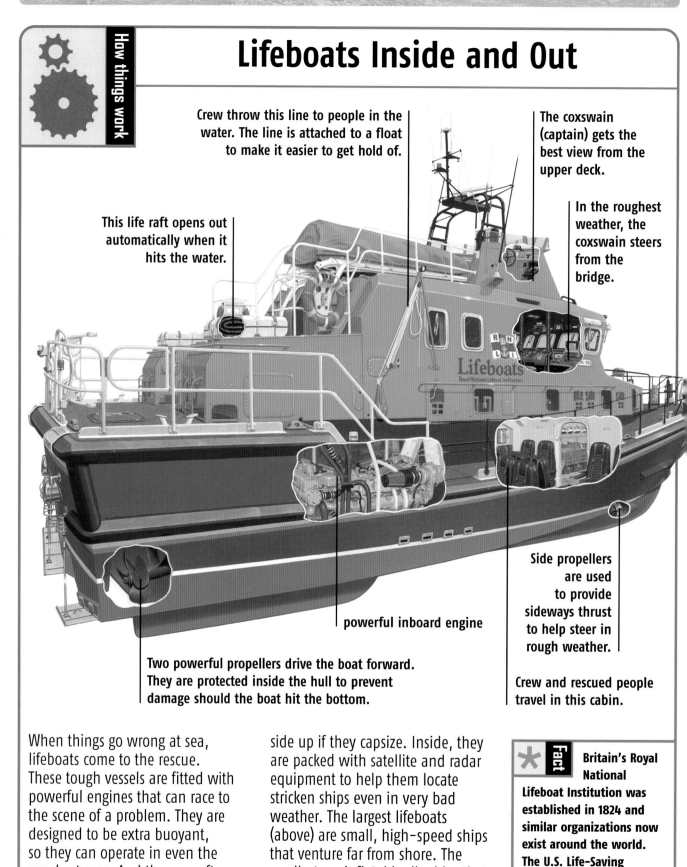

Side propellers are used to provide sideways thrust to help steer in rough weather.

Crew and rescued people travel in this cabin.

powerful inboard engine

Two powerful propellers drive the boat forward. They are protected inside the hull to prevent damage should the boat hit the bottom.

When things go wrong at sea, lifeboats come to the rescue. These tough vessels are fitted with powerful engines that can race to the scene of a problem. They are designed to be extra buoyant, so they can operate in even the roughest seas. And they are often equipped with inflatable air bags or buoyancy tanks that turn them right side up if they capsize. Inside, they are packed with satellite and radar equipment to help them locate stricken ships even in very bad weather. The largest lifeboats (above) are small, high-speed ships that venture far from shore. The smallest are inflatable dinghies that race through coastal waters, powered by an outboard motors.

★ Fact Britain's Royal National Lifeboat Institution was established in 1824 and similar organizations now exist around the world. The U.S. Life-Saving Service was established in 1871, and today it is part of the U.S. Coast Guard.

planning to build even bigger vessels that could carry as many as 14,000 containers.

Container ships are sometimes so big that they can stop only at a handful of the world's ports, known as hub ports. Once there, the containers must be unloaded and transferred to more modest vessels that will carry the goods to smaller ports. The world's busiest hub port, Hong Kong, handles around 10 million containers per year.

CARGO SHIPS

Any ship that carries goods or people could be described as a cargo ship. But in the world of modern shipping, a cargo ship is a vessel that doesn't fall into the neat categories of tanker, bulk carrier, or container ship. It is quite like a container ship, in that it can carry a mixture of packaged goods, such as automobiles, TV sets, or sacks of food. But it is also like a bulk carrier because the goods are carried in holds below deck instead of in sealed containers that sit on top. Cargo ships sometimes have their own cranes on board. The world's biggest cargo ship is currently the *Berge Stahl*. It is 1,125 feet (342 m) long and weighs 364,767 tons (328,290 metric tons).

OTHER MODERN SHIPS

General-purpose ships can be used in a variety of different ways, but specialized ships have also been developed for some jobs. Ferries that shuttle people over rivers and seas are one example. The simplest ferries are little more than large rafts made of metal. Modern roll-on, roll-off ferries are more like ocean liners with huge doors at the front and back through which vehicles drive into the ship's hold. Above the vehicle decks, there are restaurants and passenger cabins. The world's biggest roll-on, roll-off ferry, the MV *Pride of Rotterdam*, is 669 feet (204 m) long and can carry up to 1,360 passengers and 250 cars.

To save time at the dockside, roll-on, roll-off ferries have doors at both ends. If cars drive on through the stern door they disembark through the bow (below). This system means drivers do not have to reverse slowly out of the car deck.

Chain-Link Ferries

Not all ferries are designed to operate on the seas. Some carry automobiles and passengers across the mouths of estuaries where it would be impractical to build a bridge (above, in Cornwall, England). Usually the tidal currents flow quickly in places like this. To prevent them from being swept away, the ferries are designed to pull themselves along a chain that stretches along the seabed from one side of the estuary to the other. As the ferry moves along, a powerful diesel engine picks the heavy chain up from the seabed in front of it and drops it down again behind it. Only one chain-ferry operates in the United States. It is a small, hand-cranked boat that crosses the Kalamazoo River in Saugatuck, Michigan. Chain-ferries are more common elsewhere in the world.

Another specialized shipping vessel is the *trawler*—a boat or ship that brings large catches of fish into port. The smallest fishing boats have some sort of crane or other mechanism for hauling a net full of fish onboard. Large factory trawlers can clean and freeze fish the moment they are caught. This means they can fish for weeks or months at a time and bring in much larger catches.

Ships such as this often take enormous catches and are blamed by environmental groups for the collapse of fish stocks.

There are many other types of specialized vessels. Tugs are the powerful and highly maneuverable little workhorses used to tow other ships when they have no power of their own. Some tugs work in ports and others work out at sea. As their name suggests, icebreakers carve a path through the frozen seas for other ships following behind. Research ships, such as the *Glomar Challenger* and *JOIDES Resolution*, are packed with scientific instruments to help oceanographers study the seas and the marine life they contain.

A ship being built at the Cammell Laird shipyard on the Mersey River in Liverpool, England.

SHIPBUILDING

Materials and tools may have changed over the years, but shipbuilders of ancient times would still recognize many of the techniques used to construct modern ships. Unlike automobiles and trucks, ships are usually built one at a time in enormous shipyards situated in coastal regions. Once a ship has been designed, it is constructed from giant pieces called erection units that are welded together to form the overall structure. When the hull is complete, it is fitted out with its engine, electrical cables, and other equipment. After the engines have been tested, it is moved out of a dry dock into open water for sea trials.

While Britain and Germany dominated shipbuilding during the early 20th century, the East Asian nations of Japan and Korea build most ships today. A typical ship might spend 20 to 30 years at sea before being broken up for scrap. It is also quite common for ships to be converted for other uses if they prove not to be economic for their original purpose. Oil tankers have often been converted into bulk carriers, for example, and cruise liners have been converted into universities or training centers. Civilian (merchant) ships have sometimes been converted into warships, troop transporters, and hospital ships in times of war, but warships are usually designed purely as fighting vessels.

THE SCIENCE SHIP

Some of the most unusual ships ever to have been built are the research vessels used by oceanographers, the scientists who study the ocean. While most ships are designed to move swiftly across the sea and spend as little time on their voyages as possible, research vessels stay out at sea for weeks or months at a time, so the scientists on board can carry out detailed experiments.

One of the best-equipped science vessels in the world is the JOIDES *Resolution* (right), which looks like a cargo ship with a huge drilling rig sprouting from its deck. Launched in 1978, it was originally used to drill into the seabed and explore for oil. In the 1980s, it was converted into a scientific research ship. It is now used to drill out very long mud and rock samples from the seabed, so scientists can understand more about how the oceans have changed over millions of years of history. These play a key role in helping geologists, who study the materials that make up Earth, understand phenomena such as earthquakes and climate change.

The *Resolution* often drills in water more than 3 miles (5 km) deep. Its drill is not one continuous piece of metal but many bits of pipe, each about 31 feet (9.5 m) long. They are connected to form a drill "string" up to 6 miles (10 km) long. The string is lowered and raised through a 23-foot (7-m) hole in the center of the ship, nicknamed the "moon pool." This method of drilling is similar to the way an oil rig drills down beneath the ocean floor. But while an oil rig is at least anchored to the seabed, a ship can be tossed about by the waves, placing stress on the drill string and causing it to break. For this reason, the *Resolution* is fitted with a dynamic positioning system. This consists of a GPS (Global Positioning System) satellite

A scientist prepares a sonar boom that is dragged behind the ship to produce a cross-section of the rock beneath the seafloor. It does this by bouncing sound waves off the bottom and detecting the echoes.

navigation computer, and a set of 12 automatically controlled thruster engines. These are constantly firing and shutting off to ensure the *Resolution* stays in precisely the same position all the time.

The huge drilling derrick, towering 211 feet (64 m) above sea level, is the *Resolution*'s most obvious feature, but the ship has many other scientific facilities onboard. Twelve different laboratories are equipped with hi-tech microscopes, computers, and X-ray equipment. There are also precision machines for slicing up the core samples and freezing them so they can be studied in more detail in laboratories back on land.

WARSHIPS

In ancient times, there were only two kinds of ships: cargo ships and warships. Warships were generally powered by both oars and sail. The crew took up a lot of room, but they could keep the boat moving during battles, even when the wind had dropped. Cargo ships had plenty of room inside for supplies and could make longer journeys than warships but were at the mercy of the wind.

By the 15th century, sail ships had become reliable enough to be used as warships, too. The greatest warships of the age were large, fast vessels called galleons.

Galleons carried enough supplies to wage war in distant places. They ruled the waves until iron ships powered by engines were developed that could outgun and out-maneuver sailing ships.

By the 20th century, navies were equipped with huge battleships, the galleons of their days. The last U.S. battleship, the USS *Missouri*, ended its service in 1992.

MODERN WARSHIPS

In the navies of the 21st century, warships are more specialized vessels, ranging from gigantic aircraft carriers to small and fast

A Tomahawk cruise missile is launched from missile cruiser, USS Cape St. George, during the Iraq War (2003). The superstructure (upper section) of this ship has smooth sides, unlike less modern ships. This helps the ship avoid detection by radar.

USS *Indianapolis*

This cruiser saw action in the Pacific Ocean. It carried the world's first atomic bombs to the island air base used to attack Japan in 1945. A few days later, USS *Indianapolis* was sunk by a Japanese submarine. 880 crew members died, many eaten by sharks. This was the worst naval disaster in U.S. history.

1. Spotter planes were stored in this hanger. They were launched with a catapult and landed on the water beside the ship.

2. Antennae picked up enemy radio signals.

3. Engine exhaust escaped through two funnels.

4. Life rafts were present all around the ship.

5. Gun turrets could swing around to target shells. Shells were hoisted up from magazine below.

patrol boats. Cruisers are the biggest warships after aircraft carriers. They take on a wide variety of roles in the modern navy. They are mainly used in a defensive way, for example, sailing alongside aircraft carriers to protect them from enemy attack. A typical modern U.S. Navy cruiser has a crew of about 350 sailors and is armed with a variety of different weapons, including antiaircraft guns, torpedoes for destroying submarines, and long-range cruise missiles.

Destroyers are the small, tough ships that are built for speed. Originally known as torpedo boat destroyers, they were first designed to fight back against smaller boats that could speed up to ships, fire torpedoes at them, and then speed away again. When torpedo boats were replaced by submarines, destroyers became antisubmarine vessels.

Frigates are smaller than cruisers but larger than destroyers. Less heavily armed than destroyers, frigates nevertheless carry surface-to-air missiles and torpedoes. Like destroyers, modern frigates were designed to defend other ships, such as cargo vessels carrying supplies during wartime. Frigates are also used to escort landing craft carrying troops to shore.

FAST AND SLOW

Large warships play an essential role in a modern navy, but smaller, high-speed boats are no less important. A destroyer travels at speeds of more than 35 mph (56 km/h). A missile or gunboat is just a fifth of the size and can reach speeds of 58 mph (93 km/h) or more.

An important job of a navy is to help armies invade land from the sea. Large warships can get only so close to the land because of

Aircraft Carriers

The most impressive warships ever built are the enormous aircraft carriers (below). These transport not just a small fleet of airplanes but also the runway, or flight deck, used by the planes to take off and land. Catapults help fling the airplanes down the short flight deck into the air at the rate of one plane every 30 seconds. Strong steel wires stretched across the deck catch landing planes and prevent them from overshooting into the sea. The U.S. Navy operates eight huge aircraft carriers and has two more under construction, each named for a former U.S. president. Currently the biggest warships in the world, these mighty vessels are 1,092 feet (333 m) long and 252 feet (76.8) wide. Powered by onboard nuclear reactors, they can travel at more than 35 mph (56 km/h), as fast as the swiftest destroyer. Each carrier costs around $4.5 billion to build and can transport 85 airplanes and helicopters. Because an aircraft carrier's main job is transportation, it has few armaments of its own. An aircraft carrier sails with a battle groups of cruisers, frigates, and destroyers that protect it against enemy attack.

How things work

Gas Turbines

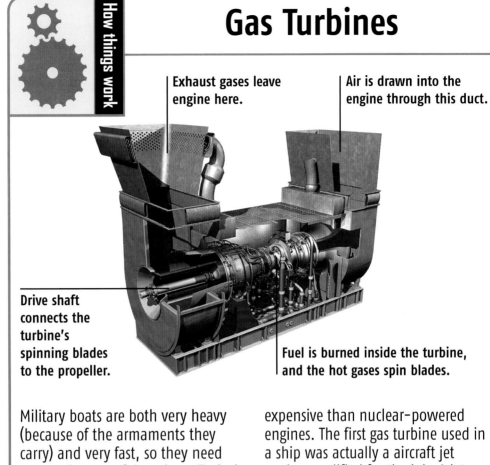

Exhaust gases leave engine here.

Air is drawn into the engine through this duct.

Drive shaft connects the turbine's spinning blades to the propeller.

Fuel is burned inside the turbine, and the hot gases spin blades.

Military boats are both very heavy (because of the armaments they carry) and very fast, so they need extremely powerful engines. Typical warships are powered by up to four gas-turbine engines and sometimes have diesel engines to help as well. Gas turbines produce power in the same way as steam turbines but are driven by hot gases instead of steam. They are simpler, safer, and less expensive than nuclear-powered engines. The first gas turbine used in a ship was actually a aircraft jet engine modified for the job. A jet airplane engine produces thrust (forward power) by burning kerosene. In much the same way, a gas turbine engine powers a warship by burning huge amounts of diesel. The gases produced spin a shaft connected to the propeller.

their huge size. They also need to stay out of range of the enemy guns. Modern navies rely on a wide range of amphibious craft (ones that operate both on sea and land) to carry troops, tanks, and other armaments from the sea to the shore. Hovercrafts, known as LCAC (Landing Craft Air Cushion) vehicles in the U.S. Navy, are extremely versatile, being able to travel over both land and sea.

However, they can carry only small loads. Large rafts called Landing Craft Mechanized or Utility (LCMs or LCUs) carry about three times as much as a hovercraft. But they have to moor in shallow water, a few feet from the beach. Landing craft such as these are carried by larger assault ships. Their job is to ferry troops and equipment to the front line, so they are fitted with few weapons of their own.

SUBMARINES

There are great advantages to traveling under the sea rather than across its surface. Military submarines have an element of surprise over ships, while scientific submarines can study much more of the ocean than vessels that have to remain on the surface. The main problem with submarines is withstanding the enormous pressure that builds up at great ocean depths.

EARLY SUBMARINES

Submarines may be among the most advanced modern vessels, but the idea behind them is a surprisingly old one. The first submarine was built in England almost 400 years ago, in 1620, by Dutch scientist Cornelis Drebbel (1572–1633). It was little more than a wooden rowboat that had been built up in an egg shape to form a completely enclosed vessel. That, by itself, was not enough to keep the water out. So the whole thing was covered with a waterproof outer skin made of waxed leather. Two rowers sat inside the craft, powering it through the water with large wooden oars that stuck out through the sides. In such a confined space, they had very little air supply, so the submarine could not remain submerged for long. Nevertheless, Drebbel's craft

World War I German submarines prepare to set out from the Baltic port of Kiel to seek and destroy enemy shipping in 1918.

successfully dived beneath the surface of England's Thames River, where it moved along at depths of 12 to 15 feet (4 to 5 m).

Better submarine designs soon followed, especially when people realized how useful they could be in times of war. Thanks to Drebbel, many early craft were

This propeller controls depth.

lamp

rudder

developed in England, but the first military submarine was an American invention. In 1776, during the American Revolution, David Bushnell (1742–1824) built a one-person submarine called the *Turtle*. It was driven by hand-cranked propellers and pumps. The *Turtle* was designed to creep up on British vessels while they were in harbor and plant mines on their hulls using a screw mechanism. However, *Turtle* never managed to sink a ship. It was not until the 19th century that more practical submarines were developed. One of the first was the *Nautilus*, built in 1800 by steamboat pioneer Robert Fulton (1765–1815). Like the *Turtle*, it was powered by the muscles of the crew, who hand-cranked a propeller. It also had a mast and sails for use when it was cruising on the surface. Built from a tough iron framework covered with a copper skin, *Nautilus* could withstand the water pressure at depths of 25 feet (7.6 m). Although it was a promising craft, no navies showed any interest in Fulton's invention.

POWERED SUBMARINES
The problem with all these early craft was that they were not really submarines, but submersibles. Submersibles are generally small,

unpowered, one-person vessels that sink beneath the water, while submarines are much larger underwater ships that move under their own power. During the 19th century, ships were powered either by sail or steam. Both, in their different ways, needed a supply of air. These power systems could operate only on the surface of the sea. There was no obvious way to power an underwater ship other than by hand.

All that changed toward the end of the 19th century with the invention of gasoline and diesel engines and electric motors. When Irish-American inventor John Holland (1840–1914) designed his first submarine in the 1870s, the U.S. Navy rejected it as too impractical. After developing four more unsuccessful submarines over the next two decades, Holland finally perfected his ideas in the *Holland VI*, launched in 1898. It was 53 feet (16 m) long and had two sources of power: a gasoline engine for surface cruising and a battery-powered electric motor for use underwater. This time the navy was more impressed. It bought the boat and renamed it the USS *Holland*. This became the first American military submarine in 1900.

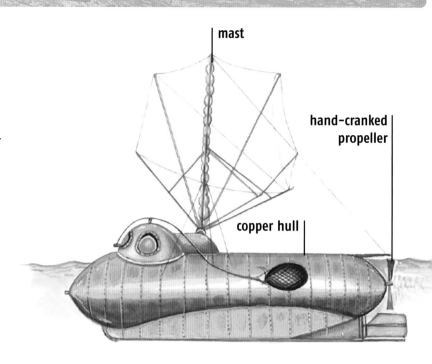

mast

hand-cranked propeller

copper hull

Nautilus designed by Robert Fulton, the U.S. engineer who also built the first successful steamboat. The submarine's mast was folded down when the vessel dived beneath the surface.

USS Holland, the U.S. Navy's first submarine, is made ready for sea. This submarine was the first to fire torpedoes through a tube, which can be seen on the bow.

Into the Deep

TRIESTE

Compared to bathyscaphes, submarines do little more than paddle in the shallows. Bathyscaphes are super-strong diving bells that descend to the very deepest points in the ocean. The record for the deepest descent into the ocean in a crewed vessel is held by the bathyscaphe *Trieste* (above). This vessel was designed by Swiss physicist Auguste Piccard (1884–1962) and his son Jacques (born 1922). The bathyscaphe had a large tank of gasoline, not for fuel, but because it is lighter than water. The crew sat in a toughened steel sphere underneath. To sink, the crew flooded a tank with water. To rise again, they released ballast (weights), making the craft lighter again. In 1960, Jacques Piccard and Lieutenant Donald Walsh of the U.S. Navy descended in *Trieste* to a depth of 6.7 miles (11 km) in the Mariana Trench, east of the Philippines, the deepest known place in all the oceans.

Holland's great rival, was Simon Lake (1866–1945). His boat *Argonaut* was the first submarine to operate in the open sea. In his career, Lake suggested 200 improvements to submarine design. He added wheels to the submarine's hull so it could move along the seabed. He developed the "even keel," which keeps a submarine steady when it dived. Lake also perfected ballast tanks, which fill with air or water to make a submarine rise and fall. Perhaps most famously of all, Lake also invented the periscope. This is a telescope fitted with mirrors that a submerged submarine's crew can use to see above the surface. (*Continued on page 68.*)

HOW A SUB WORKS

Unlike an ordinary ship, a submarine has to be able to dive into the ocean and rise again when it needs to. It has to have some way of coping with the huge pressure of the deep ocean. It also needs a way of navigating through water where it is too dark to see anything. These problems, and many more, presented a huge challenge to submarine inventors.

A crewman looks through the periscope in the control room.

DIVING AND RISING

Submarines rely on the idea of buoyancy to make them float or sink beneath the surface when they need to. Normally a submarine has positive buoyancy—it floats upward. Inside the submarine's hull there are large ballast tanks. When the submarine needs to dive, the tanks are filled with water. The submarine takes just enough water into its tanks to make it neutrally buoyant. This means it weighs exactly the same as an equal volume of water, so it neither quite floats nor quite sinks. At the bow and stern of a submarine, on the outside of its hull, are fins known as dive planes that work like an airplane's control surfaces, swiveling up and down. Once the ballast tanks are flooded, the dive planes are angled downward. As the submarine moves forward, it dives. When the submarine needs to rise, the ballast tanks are filled with air that pushes the water out. The air is stored at high pressure in onboard tanks and the dive planes are angled up.

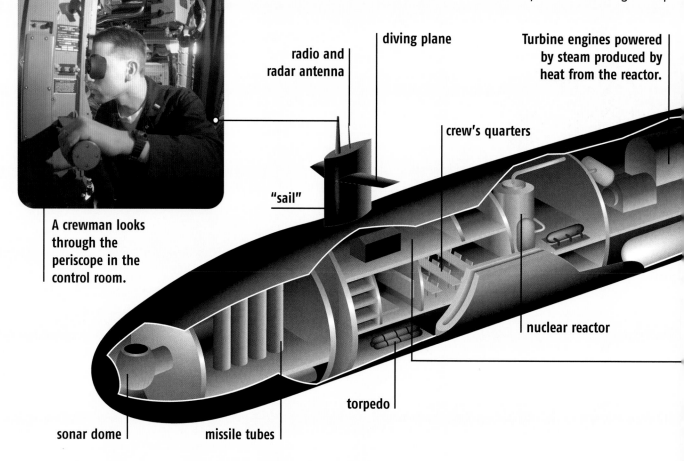

radio and radar antenna

diving plane

Turbine engines powered by steam produced by heat from the reactor.

crew's quarters

"sail"

nuclear reactor

sonar dome

missile tubes

torpedo

UNDER PRESSURE

The air inside a submarine must be kept at the same pressure as on the surface so the crew can breathe properly. Outside the submarine, the pressure exerted by the water increases with the depth. Modern submarines operate at maximum depths of about 2,000 feet (600 m), where the pressure of the ocean water is enormous. The huge difference between the pressures inside and outside would easily crush a submarine if the craft did not have a strong, double-hulled structure. In fact, every submarine has a maximum "crush depth," below which it must not dive. Inside the outer, waterproof hull there is an inner chamber, called the pressure hull. This is made from toughened steel almost 1 inch (2.5 cm) thick. The crew, the engines, and the submarine's equipment are all housed inside the pressure hull. The ballast tanks are positioned between the hulls.

FINDING THE WAY

More than a few hundred feet below the surface, seawater becomes completely dark. How, then, do submarines figure out where they are going? All modern submarines are fitted with radio and radar, but they do not work very well under water. Because sound travels much better through the ocean than light, submarines use an underwater navigation system known as sonar (*sound navigation and ranging*). This works by sending out pulses of sound and listening for the echoes that bounce off nearby objects and the ocean floor. Submarines also have inertial guidance. This uses a variety of sensors to work out the position according to how far and how fast the vessel has traveled from port. It does not rely on any visual or electronic information from outside the submarine. This process is like closing your eyes, counting your footsteps as you walk along, and trying to calculate where you are— only much more accurate!

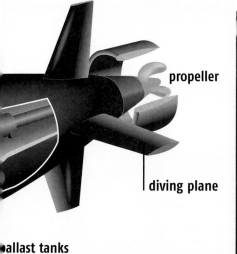

propeller

diving plane

ballast tanks

Since there are no windows, crew must steer the submarine using only instruments.

Deep Flight

With nuclear submarines costing around $2 billion dollars apiece, the future of ocean exploration is more likely to lie with low-cost submersibles such as *Deep Flight*. These sleek, one- or two-person craft can be built for as little as $5 million. That is a fraction of the cost of a conventional submarine or submersible. Launched in 1996, *Deep Flight I*

(above) was built for making undersea films. It is 13 feet (4 m) long, 8 feet (2.4 m) wide, and can carry one person lying in a prone position. Its designers are now trying to raise money to build a more ambitious submersible, *Deep Flight II*, which will be capable of traveling to the very bottom of the ocean.

SUBMARINES IN WARTIME

Despite the early promise of British and U.S. vessels, it was German submarines that first gained the upper hand in wartime. They were known as U-boats, which was short for *Unterseeboot,* or "underwater boat." They were about 300 feet (91 m) long and driven by oil-burning engines on the surface, and battery-powered electric motors while under water. U-boats were armed with self-propelled water missiles called torpedoes. During World War I

(1914–18), U-boats came close to cutting Britain off from her allies by sinking supply ships that were carrying food and weapons. Because the ships could neither spot submarines nor defend themselves against an underwater attack, the U-boats were very successful. They had sunk about 11 million tons (9.9 million metric tons) of ships by the end of the war. One of the largest casualties was the ocean liner *Lusitania*, which was sunk in 1915 with the loss of more than 1,200 lives.

During World War II (1939–45), U-boats became even more sophisticated. By this time, the German navy had perfected the snorkel, a vertical pipe that let a submarine cruise at high speed just under the surface. Invented in 1933 by Dutch naval officer Jan Wichers, the snorkel provided enough air for the U-boat's diesel engine to work when submerged. Apart from driving the submarine along, this also powered an electric generator that recharged the batteries for more deep-sea cruising. The snorkel was a very simple invention, but one that dramatically increased how long a submarine could stay under water. Other German submarine advances included acoustic torpedoes that homed in on the sound of a ship's propeller, and magnetic torpedoes that stuck onto metal ship hulls. The most advanced U-boats of the war, the Type XXI, were 250-feet (76-m) long and could dive down to 850 feet (260 m).

THE NUCLEAR AGE

Germany had led the world in submarine technology during World War II, but it was the other side who made the next major step. Once the war had ended, the United States began developing nuclear-powered submarines. The first, the USS *Nautilus*, was launched in 1955, and it soon broke all endurance records. In just six days in 1958, it covered 1,830 miles (2,945 km) in a voyage that took it beneath the ice pack of the North Pole. In another record-breaking journey in 1960, its sister ship, the USS *Triton*, made the first underwater journey around the globe.

Nuclear submarines were crucial weapons during the Cold War, a long period of high tension between the United States and the former Soviet Union that

Key inventions

Listening for Subs

transmitted sound

Echo returns to ship.

It is almost impossible to see things deep under water, because light is very quickly absorbed both by the water itself and by plankton (tiny marine life). Sound, on the other hand, travels quickly through water and can do so for very long distances. This makes it one of the best ways of detecting objects, including enemy submarines, in murky ocean waters. Detection devices either listen out for the sounds the submarines make, or they bounce ultrasound (high-frequency sound that people cannot hear) off them and listen to the echoes, using a system called sonar. Sonar equipment is fitted to submarines and surface ships (above), and helicopters also lower units into water to detect objects.

The U.S. Navy constructed a huge network of sensitive underwater microphones, called hydrophones, wired up to military bases on shore. Called the Sound Surveillance System (SOSUS), the microphone network is so sensitive that it can even tell what type of submarine is approaching. Since 1991, SOSUS has been used by ocean scientists to listen to whales and to study underwater earthquakes and volcanoes.

lasted from the 1950s until the 1990s. Both sides constructed many huge, heavily armed nuclear submarines during this time. The biggest ever built were the U.S. Ohio class, which were 560-feet (171 m) long and armed with 24 long-range nuclear missiles. But the end of the Cold War meant that many of these submarines no longer had a role to play, and most were scrapped.

RETURN OF THE SUBMERSIBLE

Nuclear-powered submarines are far too big and costly for studying the sea. Instead, oceanographers rely on a range of different underwater vessels, including small diesel-powered submarines and submersibles that are launched and controlled from ships on the surface. One of the best known scientific submersibles is *Alvin*, operated since 1964 by the Woods Hole Oceanographic Institution of Massachusetts. It is 23 feet (7 m) long and can carry

How things work

Nuclear Power

Nuclear submarines use atomic reactions to make power. When heavy atoms such as uranium split up into lighter atoms—in a process called nuclear fission— they give off huge amounts of heat energy. In a nuclear submarine, reactions such as this happen in a carefully controlled way inside an engine known as a nuclear reactor. Heat produced by the reactor is used to boil water and produce steam. The steam is then used to drive steam turbines, which turn the submarine's propellers. Steam, diesel, and gasoline engines all need oxygen from the air to burn their fuel. The great advantage of a nuclear reactor is that it needs no oxygen. This means it can operate under the water for as long as the crew have food and other supplies.

A nuclear-powered submarine cruises along the surface. There are two main types of modern military submarine. Ballistic missile subs, or boomers, like the one above carry nuclear weapons. Smaller and fast hunter-killer subs protect the boomers and hunt for the enemy.

three people on dives for ten hours at a time. While military submarines seldom go deeper than about 1,000 feet (300 m), Alvin has been used to explore to depths as great as 15,000 feet (4,500 m)—almost 3 miles (4.6 km) below the surface.

Some vessels can go even deeper than this, especially those that do not carry a human crew.

Oceanographers use *r*emotely *o*perated *v*ehicles (ROVs) and *a*utonomous *u*nderwater *v*ehicles (AUVs). ROVs are uncrewed exploration vessels controlled from a ship or other submersible by a cable, while AUVs are controlled by their own onboard computers. ROVs and AUVs are widely used by companies exploring the seabed for oil and other minerals.

People and society

Locating the *Titanic*

Many divers tried in vain to locate the wreck of the great ocean liner *Titanic* after it sank. But it was not until 1986 that U.S. ocean explorer Robert Ballard finally found the ship's remains in the North Atlantic ocean at a depth of about 13,000 feet (almost 4,000 m). No submarine can dive this deep. Instead, Ballard used the submersible *Alvin* (above) and a remotely operated vehicle (ROV) called *Jason*, attached to *Alvin* by cables, to beam pictures of the *Titanic* back to the surface. Seventy-four years after the disaster, *Titanic* was to rise to the surface once again—not as the proud ocean liner she had been, but as a still and ghostly green image broadcast on the world's TV screens.

SPORTS BOATS

Since ancient times, ships and boats have been built for either carrying cargo and passengers or to fight battles. Although speed has always mattered, it was not necessarily the most important design consideration. Powerboats used for racing and other sports, on the other hand, are designed mainly with speed in mind.

POWERBOATS
Unlike large ships, powerboats are designed to be as small, sleek, and light as possible so they can reach high speeds. While warships and submarines are made from steel, powerboats are built from strong and lightweight materials such as fiberglass or Kevlar, which is also used in bulletproof vests.

Watercraft are very popular leisure boats. They are chiefly used by vacationers, who ride them on the ocean or lakes.

72

Most powerboats have a deep, V-shaped hull that is designed to plane—rise up out of the water at high speeds. With less of the boat in the water, there is less drag (water resistance) for the engine to overcome, and it can push the hull forward at even greater speeds. Other hull designs include catamarans, which have two parallel hulls, and trimarans, with three hulls. These reduce drag by keeping a boat above the chop on the surface of the water.

Small powerboats are propelled by compact outboard motors and steered by turning a handle or wheel that swivels the whole motor. Larger powerboats have inboard engines which are inside their hulls. These boats are steered either by using a conventional rudder or a mechanism that turns the propellers from side to side.

JET SKIS

Sports boats are not always powered by outboard motors. Small one-person watercraft known as jet skis are driven by high-speed jets of water. Instead

Inside a Jet Ski

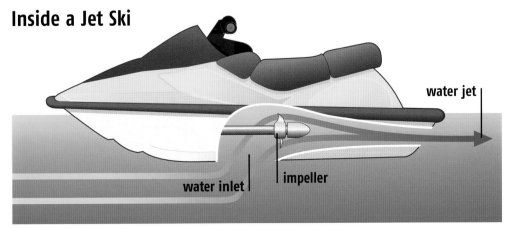

water jet

water inlet

impeller

Inside a Powerboat

How things work

Cable & Wireless Adventurer

This powerboat holds the record for sailing around the world. In 1998, the British vessel made the 28,190-mile (45,100-km) journey in 74 days and 20 hours.

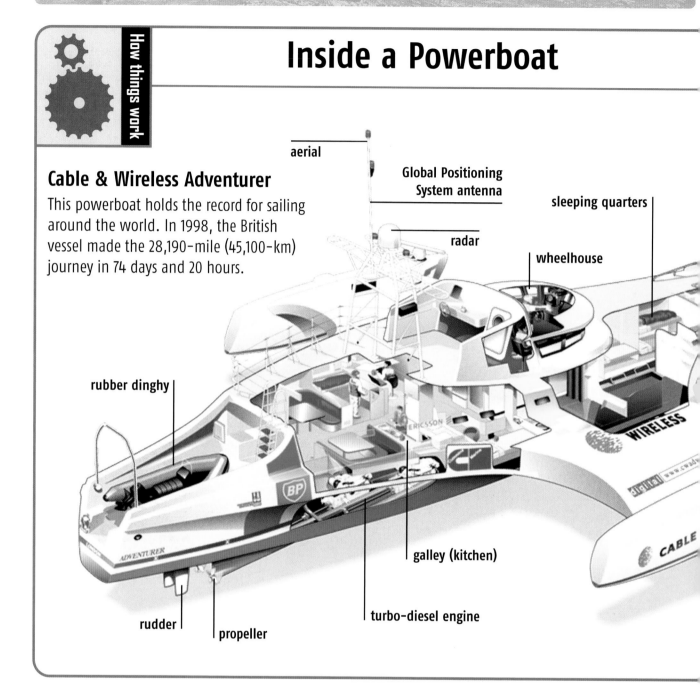

aerial

Global Positioning System antenna

radar

sleeping quarters

wheelhouse

rubber dinghy

galley (kitchen)

turbo-diesel engine

rudder

propeller

of having a propeller on the back, jet skis have a special propeller, called an impeller, inside their hulls. This sucks water in at the front of the craft and squirts it out at high speed through a hole in the back. A jet ski is steered by swiveling the direction of the water jet or by changing the force of two water jets, one on either side of the hull.

Jet skis are made from tough plastic reinforced with fiberglass. Their very buoyant hulls are designed so they always turn the right way up and never sink, even if they capsize (roll upside down). Jet skis (stand-up watercraft) and Sea-doos (craft that are sat on) were originally developed in the late 1960s by American inventor Clayton Jacobsen.

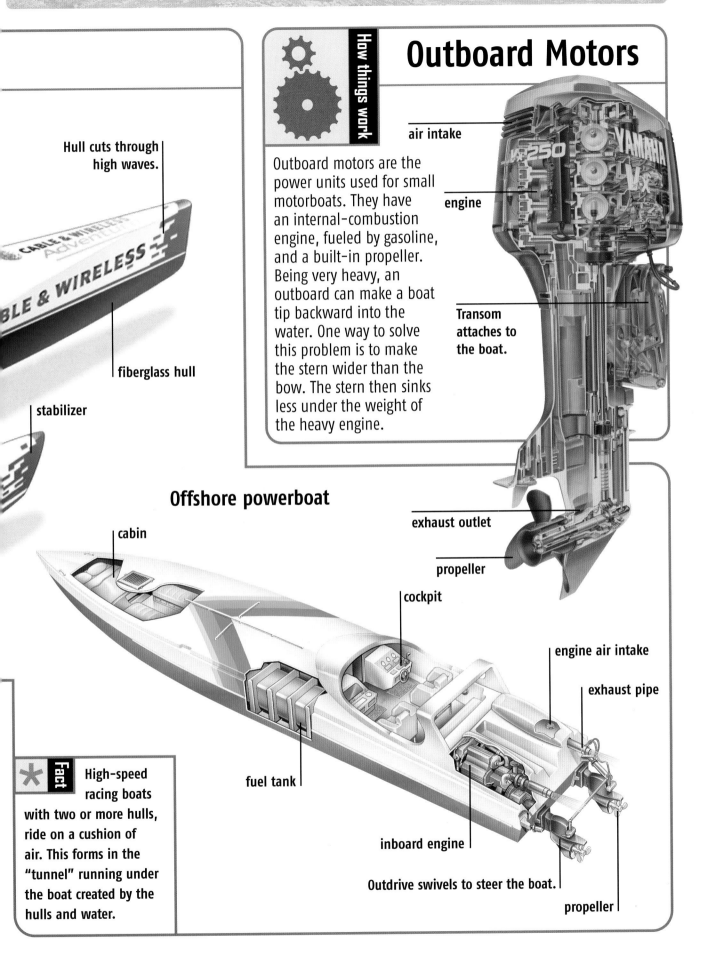

Hull cuts through high waves.

fiberglass hull

stabilizer

Outboard Motors

Outboard motors are the power units used for small motorboats. They have an internal-combustion engine, fueled by gasoline, and a built-in propeller. Being very heavy, an outboard can make a boat tip backward into the water. One way to solve this problem is to make the stern wider than the bow. The stern then sinks less under the weight of the heavy engine.

air intake

engine

Transom attaches to the boat.

exhaust outlet

propeller

Offshore powerboat

cabin

cockpit

engine air intake

exhaust pipe

fuel tank

inboard engine

Outdrive swivels to steer the boat.

propeller

Fact High-speed racing boats with two or more hulls, ride on a cushion of air. This forms in the "tunnel" running under the boat created by the hulls and water.

75

How Fast Can Boats Go?

Date	Vessel	Speed	
1807 C.E.	*Clermont* (first steamboat ferry)	4.7 mph	(7.5 km/h)
300 B.C.E.	Trireme (oar-powered ship)	6 mph	(9 km/h)
1898	USS *Holland* (submarine)	7 mph	(11 km/)
1837	*Great Western* (steamship)	10 mph	(17 km/h)
1858	*Great Eastern* (steamship)	17 mph	(27 km/h)
Today	Oil tanker	17 mph	(27 km/h)
Today	Container ship	21 mph	(33 km/h)
Today	Nuclear submarine (on the surface)	23 mph	(37 km/h)
1945	U-boat (German submarine)	23 mph	(37 km/h)
1850	Clipper sailing ships	25 mph	(41 km/h)
1907	*Mauretania* (ocean liner)	31 mph	(50 km/h)
2001	*Playstation* (sailing catamaran)	33 mph	(53 km/h)
Today	Nuclear submarine (under water)	35 mph	(56 km/h)
Today	Warship	38 mph	(61 km/h)
1897	*Turbinia* (steam turbine motorboat)	40 mph	(64 km/h)
1993	*Yellow Pages Endeavour* (sailing trimaran)	54 mph	(86 km/h)
Today	World's fastest car ferry	69 mph	(111 km/h)
Today	Hovercraft	81 mph	(130 km/h)
Today	Hydrofoil	92 mph	(148 km/h)
Today	Formula One powerboats	120 mph	(200 km/h)
1977	*Spirit of Australia* (world record holder)	318 mph	(511 km/h)

There are several different high-speed motorboat sports. Some people race around short enclosed courses in very fast but maneuverable boats, while others prefer to race across more open water in very powerful boats, like the one above.

FORMULA ONE RACERS

The fastest powerboats are Formula One (F-1) racers, which can easily reach speeds of 120 mph (200 km/h) or more. Unlike most powerboats, which have a single V-shaped hull, F-1 boats sit on a pair of narrow fiberglass catamaran hulls. These hulls keep the boat above the waves so it can move more quickly. The waves roll under the boat between the hulls. At the front, the hulls end in points called pickleforks. These help the boat rise up and speed over the surface. F-1 boats are driven by huge outboard motors.

With a sleek, aerodynamic body, Formula 1 racers look more like jet airplanes than powerboats. But one problem with their design is that they can take off into the air at high speeds. The heavy motor at the stern then makes the whole craft flip up into the air and land on its back. When this happens, an airbag inflates behind the driver's cockpit, pushing the front of the boat up, and a tank at the back of the boat fills with water, pulling the back of the boat down. Working together, these safety devices make it easier for the driver to escape.

YACHTS

Yachts are medium-sized boats used for sport and leisure. While all modern yachts have their own motors, many are really designed to be powered by sails. Smaller sail boats, such as sloops or schooners, are often called yachts as well.

Powerboats tend to be used for cruising in inland waters or for making short pleasure trips. Yachts, especially large motor yachts, are used for much longer voyages. They have an enclosed area below deck that includes basic sleeping areas and a kitchen, known as a galley.

Many yachts have been sailed around the world, often racing against each other, and are even crewed by a single person. The first yacht race took place in 1848 with permission of Britain's Queen Victoria. Originally known as the Hundred GuineasS Cup, and later renamed the America's Cup, it is the world's oldest international trophy.

A sloop is a small type of sail boat. It has two triangular sails, and it can be controlled by just one person. Sloops are only suitable for sailing close to land.

mast
spreader
boom
mainsail
jib
bow
deck
stern
rudder
centerboard
Ropes tied to cleat.

Hoverspeed Great Britain

SPECIAL VESSELS

Asked to draw a ship, most people would sketch something with an curved hull that had sails or smokestacks on top. Although most ships do indeed look like this, inventors have designed many other machines for moving people and cargo across water. The special vessels they have come up with often look and work unlike traditional ships.

CATAMARANS
Boats with a single large hull sit deep in the water and create a lot of drag (water resistance). Boats with two or three hulls, known as catamarans and trimarans, sit

much higher up, drag less in the water, and can move more quickly. Small waves pass between the hulls, which makes for a smoother ride. Catamarans are also more stable than single-hulled boats and are harder to capsize.

The fastest sailing yachts have catamaran hulls and this design is nothing new. It may have come from the South Pacific, where outriggers (small side floats) were added to dugout canoes to make them more stable. The people of islands such as Hawaii and Tonga traditionally built craft by joining two or three canoes together and suspending a sail between them.

Hoverspeed Great Britain *was once the holder of the Blue Riband trophy for the fastest crossing of the Atlantic Ocean. In 1990, the ferry took 3 days, 7 hours, and 54 minutes to make the crossing. In 1998, another catamaran ferry, from Scandinavia, took the trophy.*

In recent years, the catamaran design has been widely used on larger boats, especially high-speed passenger ferries. The world's first automobile-carrying catamaran was the 243-foot (74-m) *SeaCat*, launched in the 1980s. Powered and steered by water jets, like a jet ski, it can reach speeds of 46 mph (74 km/h). In 1990, the 100-foot (30-m) *Hoverspeed Great Britain* catamaran set a new world record when it crossed the Atlantic Ocean in less than three and a half days. The latest designs can carry up to 600 passengers and crew and 80 automobiles.

HYDROFOILS AND JETFOILS

Catamarans work by keeping more of a boat's hull clear of the water; other boats do the same job in a different way. A hydrofoil boat has wings, also known as foils, mounted on legs, or struts, beneath the hulls. As the boat picks up speed, the wings work just like those of an airplane. Water moves faster over the curved top surface of the wings than under the straight bottom. This creates a lifting force that makes the whole boat rise up out of the water and skim along on its legs. With its hull clear of the waves, a hydrofoil can speed along at 90 mph (145 km/h).

The fastest hydrofoils—known as jetfoils—are pushed along by huge water jets rather than by propellers, like jet skis and some catamaran ferries. These boats pump out around 180 tons (162 metric tons) of water each minute, which is like having 75 fire trucks on board pumping constantly.

The Boeing company has produced a number of jetfoil warships for the U.S. Navy. These have two different power sources. For cruising along at slow speeds, they have diesel engines. For racing along on their hydrofoils at top speed, they use more powerful gas-turbine engines. Although it takes a lot of power to lift a boat out of the water to begin with, hydrofoils use less power than most ordinary boats because drag on the hull is reduced.

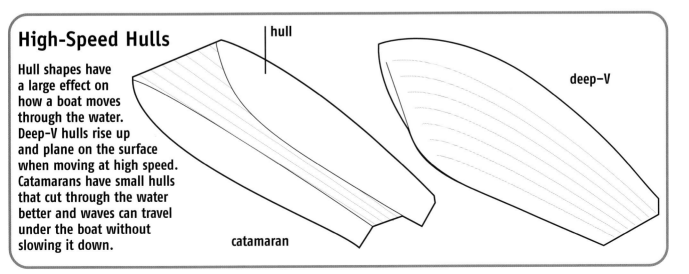

High-Speed Hulls

Hull shapes have a large effect on how a boat moves through the water. Deep-V hulls rise up and plane on the surface when moving at high speed. Catamarans have small hulls that cut through the water better and waves can travel under the boat without slowing it down.

hull

deep-V

catamaran

An experimental hydrofoil is tested by Boeing in the early 1960s. This craft was the forerunner of military jetfoils used to chase enemy submarines.

Hydrofoils were invented in 1906 by Italian engineer Enrico Forlanini. Although the German, Russian, and U.S. military tested out hydrofoils during the first half of the 20th century, the first successful hydrofoil boat, *Sea Legs*, was launched only in 1958. Jetfoils first took to the water in 1975. One of the latest catamaran designs is the *Hysucat* (*Hy*drofoil *Support Cat*amaran), a powerboat with a catamaran hull that races along on hydrofoil wings. It was designed in the 1990s by Karl-Günter Hoppe, a professor of naval engineering from South Africa.

AMPHIBIOUS CRAFT

Amphibious vehicles are designed to travel on both land and water and move easily from one to the other. The best known is the hovercraft, which rides over flat areas on a cushion of air, although there are many other designs, too.

Key inventions

Tanks that Sank

In June 1944, at the start the D-day landings of World War II, 29 amphibious U.S. tanks were launched from support ships toward the shores of France. The tanks weighed 35 tons (31.5 metric tons) each, but could float in the sea on tight canvas skirts (above). They were powered through the water using two propellers. The flotation skirts were designed to operate in calm seas, but on D-Day the waves were about 6 feet (2 m) high. Only two of the tanks made it to shore. The rest plunged to the seabed where they were finally discovered, more than 50 years later, by a team of American archaeologists.

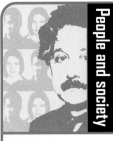

Bell's Flying Boat

Scottish-born American inventor Alexander Graham Bell (1847–1922) is perhaps best remembered for inventing the telephone. But he also experimented with agricultural machines, electricity, air conditioning, telegraph machines, kites, airplanes, and even hydrofoils. While trying to find a way of helping boats avoid minefields at sea, he came up with the idea of making a vessel that could "fly" above the waves. The boat he eventually produced, named the *Hydro Drome-4* (HD-4), was 60 feet (18 m) long and rode on four sets of hydrofoils. In 1918, HD-4 set a record speed for a hydrofoil of 70.8 mph (114 km/h). Bell's hydrofoil was so far ahead of its time that it was almost 50 years before anyone built one that could travel any faster. Like other hydrofoils, HD-4 was so fast because it traveled above the surface, and did not waste energy slicing through waves.

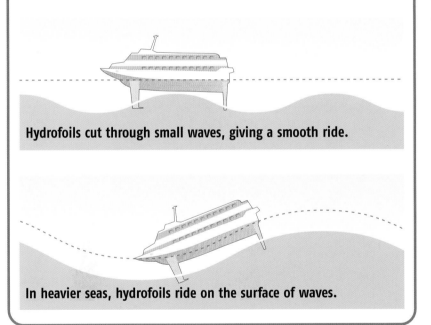

Hydrofoils cut through small waves, giving a smooth ride.

In heavier seas, hydrofoils ride on the surface of waves.

During World War II (1939–45), General Motors Corporation manufactured an amphibious six-wheel military vehicle called the DUKW, or "duck." Although it was developed from a standard truck chassis, its body looked more like the hull of a boat. On land, the DUKW could reach speeds of 55 mph (88 km/h); at sea, a single propeller pushed it along at a more leisurely 5 mph (8 km/h). Many DUKWs still survive today, more than 50 years after they were first built. In London, England, one leisure company has refurbished DUKWs and fitted them with the bodies of double-decker buses for driving tourists up and down the Thames River.

Unlike DUKWs, more modern amphibious military vehicles are usually driven by tracks. The U.S. Marine Corps' Assault Amphibian Vehicle Command Model 7A1 (AAVC7A1) is a typical craft of this kind. On land, it looks like a tank; at sea, it looks more like a boat. With an eight-cylinder diesel engine, it can travel at speeds of 45 mph (72 km/h) on land and 8 mph (13 km/h) in the water. It carries a crew of three and up to 21 combat troops.

Vehicles like the DUKW may have been the inspiration for a popular one-person amphibious vehicle called the Argo. With either six or eight powered wheels, it is one of the world's most versatile all-terrain vehicles (ATVs) and can travel on land, over snow, or through water. Unlike DUKWs, which were built from metal, Argos are made from a tough plastic called high-density polyethylene fitted to a sturdy steel frame. They do not have propellers. Instead, their tires have a special webbed design that paddles the vehicle forward or backward through water.

The Flip Ship

One of the world's most unusual vessels is *FLIP* (*Fl*oating *I*nstrument *P*latform), a 355-foot (108-m) scientific laboratory that is half ship and half submarine. It is designed to be towed across the ocean like a conventional ship. But when it arrives at its destination, the empty compartments at its narrow end are flooded with water. As the stern sinks 300 feet (91 m) down into the sea, the bow flips 55 feet (17 m) up into the air. Once *FLIP* is in a vertical position (right), it becomes a very stable place in which

to study the ocean. Since it was first constructed in 1962, *FLIP* has been used to carry out many different ocean experiments, from the way waves move through the sea to how marine animals communicate with sound. Life on board FLIP can sometimes prove challenging for the crew of 16. There are doors in the floor and tables bolted to the walls. In the bathrooms, toilets and sinks are built on both the walls and the floor. All these things ensure the crew can live happily on board the ship whether it is upright or lying down flat.

HOVERCRAFT

Some inventions have unlikely beginnings, and the hovercraft, an ingenious ship that floats on a cushion of air, was no exception. British engineer Sir Christopher Cockerell (1910–99) perfected his design for the hovercraft using two empty food cans, an air blower, and a set of kitchen scales. But when he demonstrated his hovercraft model to the British military in the 1950s, they were simply not interested. The navy insisted his vehicle was a plane, but the air force said it was a boat. When Cockerell finally convinced them that his hovercraft had potential, they classified his invention as "secret"—and promptly forgot all about it.

Cockerell was not the first person to realize that boats could travel faster on a cushion of air. More than 200 years before, in 1716, Swedish philosopher Emanuel Swedenborg (1688–1772) invented a boat that could ride on an air bubble. This was long before the invention of compact engines, so the bubble had to be maintained by a person constantly pushing air under the boat

with a specially shaped oar. Others tried to improve the design. English engineer John Thornycroft (1843–1928) tested out an air-cushion vehicle on his aunt's lily pond and patented it in 1877. But this craft, and various other designs that followed it, all suffered the same problem: how to maintain the cushion of air under the boat once they had created it?

That problem was eventually solved by Cockerell. In his hovercraft, huge fans blow air down under the vehicle where it is trapped by a large rubber skirt. This extends all the way

A U.S. Marine hovercraft zooms over the ocean. These landing craft can unload cargo on three-quarters of the world's coastline.

around the rim of the craft and drops down fully as the hovercraft begins to lift up. Small rubber "fingers" on the bottom of the skirt ensure it makes a good seal with the water beneath. Propellers mounted on the top of the craft push it along and are swiveled so the craft moves in any direction. While a hovercraft is supported by a cushion of air, that is about

A rescue hovercraft sets off across a frozen lake in Wisconsin. A hovercraft is very well suited to this environment because it can travel over both open water and ice, no matter how thin it is.

Passenger Hovercraft

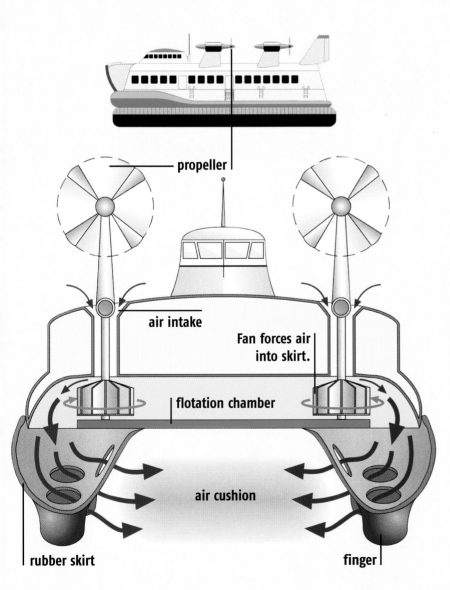

propeller

air intake

Fan forces air into skirt.

flotation chamber

air cushion

rubber skirt

finger

4 to 8 feet (1.2 to 2.4 m) thick), it also has a buoyant flotation chamber in base base to prevent it from sinking if the cushion fails.

Cockerell persuaded the British military to declassify his invention in the late 1950s so he could develop it commercially. The public were very excited by the hovercraft when it made its maiden voyage in 1959, but is was many years before the craft realized its full potential. Today, the U.S. Marine Corps relies on a large fleet of hovercraft known as Landing Craft Air Cushion (LCAC). These are used to carry troops and equipment to shore during invasions.

Some marine engineers still believe hovercraft are the boats of the future. As Cockerell himself once said: "Hovercraft will always be around—you can't uninvent something!"

INTO THE FUTURE

Ship design has come a long way since the ancient Egyptians first dipped their oars in the water. People who build boats have learned a lot in the many thousands of years since then, the ships of the future will, no doubt, look very different to those of the past. Not only will their hulls have new shapes but tomorrow's ships will also have new sources of power. Some may not even look like ships at all.

OVER THE WAVES

Lifting a boat clear of the waves makes it travel much faster. The latest ship designs try to achieve this but in very different ways.

Like modern car ferries, the latest warships use catamaran or trimaran hulls to speed themselves over the waves. In 2000, the U.S. Navy and Britain's Royal Navy began testing an innovative new trimaran warship called the RV (Research Vessel) *Triton*. Its trimaran design has a whole range of advantages: It allows ships to be longer but still inexpensive to build. It makes them more stable, faster, and creates a large deck surface for carrying airplanes or amphibious landing craft.

Another design similar to a catamaran is called SWATH (Small Waterplane Area Twin Hull). The waterplane of a boat is the part

Sea Slice is a SWATH ship designed to travel at more than 30 mph (48 km/h) in waves as high as 12 feet (3.5 m).

Conventional Vessel

SWATH Vessel

that actually cuts through the water. Engineers have found they can make large SWATH boats that are stable even at very high speeds by making the waterplane as small as possible using a pair of very slender hulls. Unlike in a catamaran, where the hulls ride on the water, the hulls of a SWATH boat are under water and the deck rides high above them. This makes the boat faster because only a small part of it is in contact with the waves. The ideas behind SWATH designs date back to 1880.

A very small amount of the hull of SWATH vessels is in contact with the waves. The up and down motion of the waves has less of an effect on the SWATH hull compared to a conventional V-shaped design.

How things work

Water and Magnets

One of the most promising new designs for a ship engine uses *magnetohydrodynamics* (MHD). This long complicated word simply means using the power of magnetism to make water move.

MHD engines first came to widespread attention in 1992 when they were tested on a propeller-less Japanese ship called the *Yamato 1* (above). Because they have no moving parts, MHD craft are much quieter and more efficient than conventional engines.

In an MHD engine, seawater is passed through a chamber known as a thruster tube. An electric field and a magnetic field also pass through the tube, acting at right angles to one another and to the direction of the water current. The salt in the seawater makes it conduct electricity. This makes the water interact with the electric and magnetic fields in a way that speeds up the flow. A MHD ship sucks water in at the front and pumps it out at a higher speed at the back, a little like a jet ski.

Neither ships nor airplanes are perfect modes of transport. Airplanes are fast but carry only small amounts of cargo, while ships can carry huge loads but only at much slower speeds. Some engineers are now trying to combine the best of both worlds in a type of combination of ship and airplane known as a Wing in Ground Effect (WIG) boat. Like a hovercraft, it flies just above the water on a cushion of air; like a boat, it can carry huge loads; and like a plane, it can fly at high speeds. WIG boats are now being developed for both commercial and military uses.

POWER TO THE FUTURE

From oars to steam engines and from sails to nuclear power, ships have been driven in many different ways over the last few centuries. Most modern ships rely on diesel engines. But if oil becomes more expensive or starts to run out, as many people believe it will, new types of power will need to be found. Some leisure boats, such as the *Sol 10 Suncruiser*, are already powered by large solar panels that make energy from sunlight. Solar-powered boats can reach speeds of only 4 to 5 mph (5 to 8 km/h) at the moment, but greater speeds may be possible in the future.

Throughout their long history, ships have made more use of the wind than of any other power source. Innovative new wind-powered generators are now being developed to make electric power on land. Could similar designs find their way onto ships, too? In the

A solar-powered boat works by converting the energy in sunlight into an electric current, which powers a motor. The energy conversion is performed by a panel of solar cells.

Invisible Ships

The "stealth" technology used to make fighter planes invisible to radar is also being used on ships. The specially absorbent materials that cover a stealth ship's hull make these vessels appear to be much smaller on an enemy radar screen. The U.S. Navy's *Sea Shadow* (which also has a SWATH hull) was the first ship to be designed in this way. It was originally tested in secret at nighttime, before finally being revealed to the public in 1993.

In fall 2002, the U.S. Navy began tests of a Norwegian-built Stealth boat called the *Skjold* (above). This a word means "shield" and is pronounced "shold." With a top speed of about 60 mph (100 km/h), it is much faster than the *Sea Shadow*. It is also a very high-tech boat. There are more than 40 computers on board, so much of the boat is automatic and it needs only around half the crew of a traditional patrol craft.

1920s, German aircraft engineer Anton Flettner (1905–62) invented a new type of sail made of rigid material that rotated in the wind. The idea was rediscovered in 1985 by French ocean explorer Jacques Yves Cousteau (1910–97) on his ship *Alcyone*, which was named for the daughter of the Greek god of the wind. Using two 33-feet (10-m) high rotating "turbosails," as he called them, Cousteau cut the fuel consumption of his boat's engine by as much as a third while greatly increasing its overall power and speed. Turbosails and other wind-catching devices have been added to other ships but have yet to catch on.

Over two thirds of Earth's surface is covered by water, so people will always need ships and boats. The vessels of tomorrow are likely to be bigger, faster, and safer than those of today. Some may look more like planes than boats and others may be powered by the Sun or wind. However they turn out, ships will always harness Archimedes' principle in the same way as the simplest dugout or raft.

Time Line

5000 B.C.E.
Mesopotamians
invent sails.

3000 B.C.E.
Egyptians invent
wooden-planked boats.

1000 B.C.E.
Phoenicians make the first
major ocean voyages.

1620 C.E.
Cornelis Drebble
launches the first
submarine.

1819
USS *Savannah*
makes first steam-
powered voyage
over the Atlantic.

1836
Francis Pettit
Smith and John
Ericsson invent
the propeller.

1897
Charles
Parsons uses
steam turbine
to drive
Turbinia.

c.5000 B.C.E.

1600

1900

250 B.C.E.
Archimedes explains the
science of buoyancy.

1818
Packet ships
start first
regular service
across the
Atlantic.

1886
Gottlieb
Daimler
launches
gasoline-
powered boat.

1783
The first steam-
powered boat,
the *Pyroscaphe*,
is launched
in France.

90

1906
Enrico Forlanini invents the hydrofoil.

1955
USS *Nautilus* becomes the first nuclear-powered submarine.

1960
Trieste bathyscaphe makes a record breaking dive to the bottom of the ocean.

1977
Ken Warby sets the world water speed record of 318 mph (511 km/h).

1993
U.S. Navy reveals the first stealth boat, *Sea Shadow*.

1990

1912
Titanic sinks after striking an iceberg.

1959
Christopher Cockerell launches the first practical hovercraft.

1956
The first container ship, *Ideal X*, is launched from New Jersey.

2004
Queen Mary 2, the world's largest ocean liner, makes first voyage.

1992
Yamato becomes the first vessel to use a magnetohydrodynamic engine.

1986
Robert Ballard discovers the wreckage of the *Titanic*.

Glossary

amphibious A vessel that can travel on both water and land.

bathyscaphe A submarine that can dive to great depths.

bireme An ancient warship with the oars arranged on two levels.

boat A small watercraft.

bow The front of a ship.

bulkhead An internal wall that divides the inside of a ship into watertight compartments.

buoyancy The way that some things naturally tend to float.

carvel built A method of building a ship with smoothly joined wooden planks.

catamaran A ship with two hulls.

clinker built A method of building a ship with overlapping wooden planks.

clipper A fast sailing ship.

composite A ship made from a combination of wood and iron.

dhow An Arab sailing boat.

dugout A canoe made by removing the wood from a trunk.

gas turbine A powerful engine that burns fuel continuously in a combustion chamber.

galley A sailing warship.

hovercraft An amphibious craft that floats on a cushion of air.

hull The main body of a boat.

hydrofoil A boat that flies along on underwater wings called foils.

junk A type of Chinese boat.

lateen A triangular sail that can drive a boat toward the wind.

magnetohydrodynamic A type of engine that uses magnetism and electricity to power a ship.

outboard A compact motor and propeller used on powerboats.

rudder A swiveling board at the back of a ship used for steering.

ship A large watercraft (usually bigger than a boat).

stealth A way of making military ships invisible to radar.

stern The rear of a boat.

steam turbine A type of engine driven by a jet of steam.

submarine A ship that travels mostly underwater.

SWATH Small Waterplane Area Twin Hull, a type of boat with two hulls that has very little area in contact with the water.

trimaran A three-hulled boat.

trireme An ancient warship with the oars arranged on three levels.

Further Resources

Books

Introduction to Naval Architecture by E. C. Tupper. Butterworth-Heinemann, 1996.

The Complete Idiot's Guide to Submarines by Michael DiMecurio and Michael Benson. Alpha Books, 2003.

Web Sites

Smithsonian: Aviation and Transportation

http://www.si.edu/science_and_technology/aviation_and_transportation/

U.S. Navy

http://www.navy.mil

Index

Page numbers in **bold** refer to feature spreads; those in *italics* refer to picture captions.

Picture Credits